DEVOTIONS and DESECRATIONS on the DOWNTOWN BUS

or
M-15 MADRIGAL
a poetic memoir

by

JD RAGE

edited by Ptr Kozlowski

Venom Press
New York, NY

Devotions and Desecrations On The Downtown Bus
A Poetic Memoir by JD Rage
Edited by Ptr Kozlowski

ISBN 978-0-578-90352-1 (paperback)
ISBN 978-0-578-90352-8 (eBook)

39 of these poems were previously published
in the chapbook *Devotions & Desecrations Book I*
© 1999 JD Rage and Venom Press
13 of these poems were published
in the journal *Stained Sheets*,
edited by Bruce Weber
© 1996 through 2006 JD Rage

Cover and book design by Ptr Kozlowski
Bus_LED font by AlanRF
https://fontstruct.com/fontstructions/show/1516690
licensed under a Creative Commons Attribution license
Text set in Linux Libertine
licensed under the SIL Open Font License, Version 1.1.
https://www.fontsquirrel.com/license/linux-libertine

Back cover photo of JD Rage by Robert Butcher

Venom Press
New York, NY
JD Rage and Jan Schmidt, co-founders
Ptr Kozlowski and Jan Schmidt, editors
venompressnyc@rantrecords.com

CONTENTS

Introduction

by Jan Schmidt

The first time I met JD was in 1981 at her apartment on Fifth Street in the East Village. She and I became friends till her passing on March 3, 2018. We ran around the Lower East Side, played in bands, and wrote fiction and poetry. In the band, JD Rage wrote most of the songs and sang while playing the bass, with Ptr Kozlowski and me on guitars, and Hazel Lucchesi on drums.

Link to information on bands can be found here:
https://www.rantrecords.com

In the 1990s JD and I co-founded Venom Press and published a number of chapbooks and nine issues of our literary magazine, *Curare*, which are digitized on my website at
https://www.janschmidt-writer.com

No matter what was going on in JD's life, she was always writing poetry. Powerful, accessible, angry, and then, out of all that pain, a moment of rapture would pop up. She and I always spoke about publishing her group of poems that she referred to as her *Bus Poems*. I'm sorry we didn't do this before she passed, but I'm sure she'd be pleased to see them come out now. They comprise a fantastical yet realistic picture of New York City in the 90s as well as the decade in JD's life before she got terribly sick and had to retire from her job early—so no more *Bus Poems*. But she never stopped writing. I can see her now, up there in the clouds, in black leather, studs and band pins on her wings, declaiming her poems to her angels of desolation.

Editor's Note

On a to-do list for a Saturday in March 1996 JD Rage included "locate poetry notebook so I can continue M-15 Madrigal". It was almost two years since she had conceived this project and wrote Devotion #1. Finding herself no longer able to walk to work, she had decided to put her bus rides to good use and write a poem each work day. But events had intervened, notably her buying her own apartment and moving into it. She was still unpacking that Saturday, but she found the notebook and Monday morning resumed the bus poems in earnest. She had said there would be 240 or more, perhaps because that's about how many work days there are in a calendar year. From March 11, 1996 to May 14 the following year, she wrote 240 (#2 through #241). After reaching that milestone on a Wednesday, she started the next morning, on the next page, with Desecration #1. But her pace eased up. She wrote the 45 poems in the Desecrations series over the next ten months.

JD Rage was a multitalented person who lived a complex life. Here are 286 glimpses of what parts of it were like.

Ptr Kozlowski

Devotion # 1

Charles Bukowski is dead
this news Ptr writes
from San Francisco
Crime on the buses is up
that was on the radio
17 teenagers beat up
one of their own
yesterday
on a bus
I am on the bus
I have a million enemies
that I want to get
before they get me
Charles Bukowski
beat himself up
though maybe not usually
on a bus
if it hadn't been for the booze
he might have been one of
those guys who live forever
he went to places where
he could get into bar brawls
as a prelude to
listening to records of
the symphony
and painting pictures
and dreaming of sexpot
temptresses and
bottles of cold beer
it's not a bad way to go
unless you want to
die on a bus
like I do

Sunny morning movie crews
block the sidewalk on Houston
between A & B
regular workers trying
to get to work are of
no concern
One director type jumped
in the air when I slammed by
brushing his back roughly
surprised that anyone
would challenge his high position
in the middle of the walkway
good for you - you fuck

Bus pulls in
less than a five minute wait
can't look toward the East River
the sun is overruling everything
in that direction turning it
into a golden washout
Chinese truckers are worse
than movie people, they
won't move at all for the bus
we come so close we nearly
shear off the driver's door
one bus window is loose
and flaps like a bird wing
in the wind
I enjoy the cold fresh air
it cuts the morning scent of
garlic, toothpaste, Listerine and
strong perfume.

Sleepwalking late to the M-15
I find myself barreling
down Allen Street toward
undesired destination -- work
morning sunlight is high
like 1:00 PM instead of 7:30 AM
Soon we'll be thrown back into
darkness at this hour
but today I feel a thrill as
my body interprets
the status of the light and air
as being late for work
a reminder of times I
came in straight from the
after-hours joints
immediately downing
three cans of orange soda
from the coke machine
upon arrival
drinking all three at once
to cure my alcohol induced
dehydration

Everyone seems happy
wearing new spring clothes
they received at Christmas

The last remnant
of tight zipper
tight scarf bundle
two pairs of socks
boots with salt stains
is blowing away in
spring's chill breeze

4

So nervous today
the bus is late
"go in and come right out,"
says the dispatcher
"I see her, she's behind me,"
the driver tells him
the dispatcher makes notes
in his book
heavy machinery
huge long trucks
with giant 50 foot poles
dump trucks that
thunder over metal slabs
covering road construction
I feel like bricks are jumping
inside my chest
buses are only late
when I need to get
someplace without fail
at a certain time
today I will be going
to Long Island for a meeting
can't miss my ride
it will be a long drive

cop cars more trucks
Chinatown trucks
unloading at 7:23 AM
junkies turned
methadonians congregate
outside their center on
East Broadway
they are more nervous
than I am
some need their fix
some will pretend to drink

and will spit back their dose
and sell it
for cocaine money
spring is coming
the drug eats at their bones
my bones hurt in
this churning bus
as it rampages
down our potholed
excuse for
pavement

5

I am finally on the bus
I was wondering if I might die
before it arrived
one was pulling away as I
approached the stop
I feel so tired
my natural inclination is
to fall over
land flat on my face
someday soon I will do it
I'm so weak from this day
and sickness
I can't believe I'm on my feet
at all -- I feel my eye sockets
artificially extended
my eyes or whatever medium
I am seeing through hazily
are somewhere under my
cheekbones
high and flat -- the only vestige
of my distant Creek heritage
other than all the common

Native American physical ailments
I'm going to a funeral
tomorrow - very glad it isn't mine
I must plan my burial and
write my will or
stop heading so rapidly toward
my grave

6

I ran for the bus
this morning at 6:57 AM
I wanted to get some work done
before the funeral
the driver waited for me
when she saw me
running down Allen Street
and even said "good morning"
out my window
pallets with deliveries are
stacked high
and Asian men
sip from steaming coffee cups
standing around behind
their trucks
on a break already
or maybe it's their last
break before
quitting time

we made it express
to Catherine Street
my ride today clocked in
at five minutes
it was a bumpy one
there were no shocks on

this bus
if you don't
include the
riders

7

Coming in late today
I don't feel good
I have a vampire bite
on my left leg
my back is killing me
my teeth are not long
for this world
some riders are reading magazines
or doing paperwork
most are looking out the window
at the gray day hovering
above Delancey Street
The Williamsburg Bridge
is shrouded in a huge sheet
of white gauze
a black pigeon watches us
from the imitation gaslight
in the Allen Street Park --
a narrow strip of fenced
land running down the middle
of Allen Street
the park benches have had
their slats removed
a park that languishes
between two continuous streams
of heavy delivery trucks
covered in noxious fumes
a park that only bums
who live in the open air

or under cleverly constructed
tents of plastic and cardboard
like human hermit crabs
and junkies of the most
decrepit ilk can tolerate

we're passing through
Chinatown now
heading once again
for antiseptic downtown tomb

8

It's a smooth morning
cars move around the corner
I cross between them
and arrive just as
the bus door opens to
let me in
smooth as a water ballet
massive trucks
pirouette beneath the
green tinged stands of trees

I saw a bud on the forsythia
everything is budding
I hope they don't fall off
in the cold
heavy rain is predicted by noon
and it will continue to be cold
even though
spring arrives on Friday

my skin is smooth too
I have started to take care

of things
maybe too late
but I will go down with
smooth skin
the trucks and I will
twirl into dust

9

Spring comes in
under polluted
bad weather skies
the trees are still
looking like skeletons
some with a little
green fuzz
open-coated school girls
brave the chill air
daring winter
to touch them
again
as they stroll
with heads down
in less than five minutes
we are already in front of
the Golden Unicorn
in Chinatown
we take the big turn
down Worth
to City Hall

older polyestered
Asian women
do Kung Fu
exercises in the children's
playground
it's so warm

they are out
in force today
but there is
not a single young person
in sight

10

Old broken down stumble bums
of all racial persuasions are
excited and inspired by the very
sight of me haphazardly breaking
into their alcoholic DTs
something galvanized the white one
with his fading seediness
resembling the acquired look
of a young skinhead boy
but probably he just shaved
in the men's shelter to
chase away the lice
at least the real ones
something urges him to
address the stony silence
of my profile
"hey girl over there"
he is cheerfully waving a
pint of brand X vodka

"hey poetry girl"
-- I having reached the
stage in life where I
am hardly a poetry
or any other kind of
girl --
I don't answer
but instantaneously reach
my boiling point

watching him guzzle that
booze and not give up
his quest
"Wake-up girl! Is anybody
home? he yells happily
into the quiet poetry reading
space

I want silence now
and I am jealous
I want to grab his bottle
and run with it forever
So I get up and leave
give him my raging back
"say, I don't have to deal with
no drunken assholes today"
I rasp on my way out
the door

after work I decide
to take the bus home
so I sit down on the wall
that separates Trinity Church
and its thin cracking grave markers
from the downtown masses
I am waiting for the M-9
coat open, hood up to cut
the spitting rain, a bag with
my new computer modem toy
at my side when the black one
approaches
he stands too close

when there is lots of room
his foot is near my bag
he is rapidly talking to himself
I move the bag and inch myself
down the wall a bit

to reclaim my personal
space for which the necessity
is eliminated in demonic alcohol
intoxication and cocaine injection
he uses my movement
and the fact that I am white
against me
attacking with that old line
about why do I assume because
he's black that he will
steal all my possessions
He leans and bends his raggedy
self down and spits with the rain
his soft swearing that nobody else
can hear
"you damn uppity bitch" he whispers
"you damn cocksucking white mess, why
you always..."
I get up pissed off
I have nowhere to stomp out of this time
I only sat down because my back hurt
I was already downwind of a chain smoker
I was already miserable enough
the ragman blocked my view of the
horizon where I could see if the bus
was approaching
I begin to feel like I am under suspicion
I start to get bigger
every motion is an emotion
a magnification of itself

three diminutive gray panther ladies
are watching now
I am hoping they will curl up their
blue-haired frames and jump him
intervene -- protect -- insulate me
from this part of reality

The M-1 arrives
this man is hoping I will get on
I can read his projected desires
in my schizophrenic mind
because he knows I am the perfect target
he knows he got to me --
cracked the barrier between us
but it was move or punch him out
emaciated ash colored tall blackness
in stained tan parka
a feathery skeleton
he would have been pulverized
he might have felt what I did
when he and the white faux punk alkie
ruthlessly decimated my importance

I disappointed him since I'm going
to Avenue B and Houston on the M-9
he peers out of the smoky bus window
scowling and sputtering at the universe

when finally I looked away
and gave up trying
to pretend his invisibility or mine
I saw the wild gray ghostbusters cosmos
flying darkly over City Hall
and realized that
at least the sky is
beautiful

11

Low hanging
ominous white cloud
encircles Avenue A building
amid a sky of otherwise
solid gray

the bus is late
as usual there are three
to South Ferry before
a solitary City Hall
good thing I only have
mild schizophrenia
or this repeated pattern
of bus arrivals might hold
a more treacherous
meaning for me

the buildings all have
two signs
mystical looking
Chinese characters
over Hing Hing Market
Young Wing Inc.
Kin Wah Bakery
Number One Long Hing
Market Inc.
and the windows are all
decaled with larger
Chinese writing
there are many wedding stores
hovering over East Broadway
on the second story
and the Law Offices
of Gim C. Wong

every morning
the Chinese grandmothers
make me feel guilty
as they do their
slow motion exercises
in the park
they do arm thrusts that look
like elegant Karate moves

I watch them
from the bus
riding when I
should be
walking

12

Friday
I am full of pain
my spine feels cracked
and damaged
medication makes me dull
last night it put out
my lamp -- the light
but not the burning
and today it has returned
in full force
in my back
so bad that
this bus ride can make it
no worse

My brain is dull
all good ideas from
yesterday have hazed out
I didn't even test
my new computer modem
but curled up on
my burgundy couch
in a very strange position
to remove the pressure
as I went into a medicated
loop de loop

I dreamed that I
played with Elvis the parrot
like he was a cat
he never bit me in
that dream

13

Riding into dark
sky - rain last night
everything cleansed
in it wake
another cold spring
day ahead
my back felt mangled
for ten days
but now is tolerable

I ran out of
psychiatric medication
(Wellbutrin) due
to new prescription Catch 22's
inspired
by Republican cost cutting
with no regard to the
consequences
to the human spirit
which is free
why can't they just
admit drugs are worth
only 2 cents each
reduce the price
instead of denying
expensive chemical concoctions?

Five minute ride to work

is over
why is it that it takes
very little time to get
to places you don't want to go
and a lifetime to finally
reach the places that you do?

14

7:50 AM
It's going to be
a weird day
I am late - forgot to set
the alarm
probably Monica is dying

Oil delivery is being made
at the bus stop
I breathe five minutes
of fumes
I will go to
another funeral today
if I can't avoid it
we've had two sets of three
I hope the string of deaths
is over
but somehow
I think not
it is cold again
more like winter than spring
and windy
the sun is not capable
of warming anything up
today

Cold morning
snow is predicted again
Am I in NYC or is this
some alternate reality
instigated by a fallen angel
with a warped reaction to
to earthly hijinks
deep freeze NYC
the angel chorus rises
frozen humans
have no energy to engage
in murder
it is hard to rob
in frigid weather
fingers could fall off
before the lock is picked
most of us can stay inside
if we want to
but it's been a long winter
for the trees and pigeons
the squirrels in the projects
the rats down in the sewer
homeless in the subway stations

subway stations smell of urine
my building foyer smells of urine
angel -- if you're really there
-- why don't you send some
spring rain to wash these
smells away?

Today is March 29th
deja vu on me
because I thought yesterday
was March 29
I hate doing this day
over
God is puking on us
Before reaching my
M-15 stop (a 5 short
blocks from home)
I was hit with
alternating
sleet, rain, hail & snow
and then all four at
once
the weatherman said
"we have your basic
schmutz out there folks"
before boarding
for trip downtown,
I saw a giant hail stone
bounce off
the big butt of
a trainee bus dispatcher
who was leaning in
his boss' car window
it sprung up off his blue
sweatsuit and flew way into
the air -- the dispatcher
finished his conversation
and went to take up his
post on Allen Street
when he turned around
I saw his face was
handsome

I wonder if
today I will be
an April Fool
they are unloading boxes
of Ho King Broccoli
near Canal Street
I wonder if I eat
Ho King Broccoli

Many people are
lined up early
for their Methadone
today
I wonder why I was
allergic to Methadone
and puked from 14th Street
all the way to Coney Island
These people all
have sunken cheekbones,
wan pallors and slightly
stooped posture
I wonder why they
are still so attractive
to me

18

As always I am
very concerned about
the weather in the morning
comfort and staying well
are my objectives
yesterday

John McSherry
dropped dead
while umpiring
an opening day
baseball game --
collapsed on the field
gone within an hour
he weighed over 300 pounds
that may have been
what punched his ticket
but I prefer the
destiny theory
I like to think
that a person goes when
the time comes
and even suicides
are included
their time was up
and they knew it
in some ways
(or in many ways)
McSherry's death could
have been labeled
suicide by fork and spoon
in the wake of metabolic
imbalances that he
ignored
or did baseball kill him
with a feast of junk food
I don't think
veggie burgers, turkey hot-dogs
on 7 grain buns,
lowfat ice cream or
lite beer are served
at the stadium concession
stands
or it could have been
the cold weather

now that greedy owners
start the season before
spring has taken hold
across the country
-- the Yankee opener in
Cleveland was snowed out --

I used to be a baseball fan
I was content to dream
of playing center field
replacing Mickey Mantle
now the Mick is dead
killed by alcoholic infatuation
and his memory
stands accused of
using influence to get
himself a new liver
which didn't help him anyway
and it isn't quite so
simple to be happy.

19

my memory is going --
last night
I almost burned down
my new apartment
cooking rice and beans
sautéing onions --
left them blackening
in the frying pan
while I worked at
my computer --

I am in a fog
of high blood sugar
my hangover from
yesterday's fling
with poor eating habits

my CD ROM drive
kept me up past
midnight
refusing to work
even after being fed
new software products

I felt so weird
in the night
I can't even describe it
but sort of like
I was a machine
made of metal
like this bus
and cold inside
like this morning
Easter is coming
a plane went down
last night
killing a close friend
of the president
all meetings conferences
and coup d'etat are
cancelled until
tomorrow

21

City Hall is smiling at me
her mouth is wide open
lit by spotlights
raised on eyebrows of
three draperies lined up in a row
over tall banks of windows
she sticks out her tongue
an imaginary red carpet tumbling
down granite stairs
between
toothy columns
In spite of how she mocks me
now
I think of all the dirty deals
corruption
maybe even plots to kill
she has harbored in her gut
In spite of her undesirable
history in a rough neighborhood
the golden glow
bathed in Nature's artistry
heightened by
the cold crisp atmosphere
makes her elegant
makes me wish she was something
I could be proud of.

22

Dark and cold Good Friday
little drops of rain a nuisance
on my glasses but not enough
to break out an umbrella

I almost smash into
an exiting passenger on the M-15
who is dressed in black
the front overhead lights
of the bus are not working
so I didn't see anyone
I was simultaneously leaping
awkwardly up from the curb
so nearly broke a leg
getting out of the way
I always seem to be
getting out of someone's way
people who barrel down the sidewalk
without looking
bus riders who pop
out of darkened doorways
bike riders, skateboarders, speed
skaters
people flying out of the elevators
What? Am I so polite?
Or am I just invisible?
One day I will stop caring
what happens and everyone
will have to move for me.

23

Bad Chinese lunch
at crummy new fast food
right where my old favorite used
to be
which in comparison
makes it worse
than if it was just an ordinary
lousy lunch

the sidewalks are clear

but it is nasty out
my fingers are frozen
mini-Popsicles
all this mess we have now
and still call the weather
fits in nicely with my theory
that rocket ships have
incited Nature to devour
herself
almost like a virus has been
sucked through the ragged
fuel blistered atmospheric
holes we are punching out
causing bad storms
mysterious varieties of ugly
growths on earth's
creatures and
other sundry manifestations

I was born on July 11, 1947
at the time of the first recorded alien
invasion of the USA in modern times
I could be one of them
A space visitor, an intergalactic intruder
but to get real, I must have been
conceived in October of 1946
which makes me a Scorpio
like I always knew I was anyway
so there you have it
I am either a space monster
or a Scorpio
both entities being problematic at best

I consider myself to have been alive
at the time of conception
either here or in the wild yonder
that certainly explains why
I am so much in favor of abortion
but I do wonder if the US Space

Program can be blamed for
the recent rash
of bad Chinese fast foods
in lower Manhattan
or am I just being paranoid?

24

I reset the alarm clock
4 times this morning
it being the second day of
daylight savings time
but here I am on the
downtown bus
with not much daylight to save
cold still
Chinatown unloaders are wearing
heavy gloves
their white vehicles are closed
up tight
waiting for a warmer afternoon
our bus window
is fogged with raindrops
outside people in winter coats
people coming on the news saying
they can't take it no more
trucks are double parked
along East Broadway
All of us are waiting for Spring

25

I make the morning darker
by wearing sunglasses
once used to hide my soul

now a symbol of hope
that some morning
the sun will shine
more snow is on the way
it seems
it will come until we believe
that it will never stop
I am comfortable
with my new apartment
and I rarely think of
519 and Billy Demon
who once chased me
totally naked down
East 5th Street
as I left for work
I took the subway then
now I can hardly bear it
I have never had a real boyfriend
But since it's Spring
despite the rotten weather
things are wakening up in me
with the more strength
than in many years
ordering me to stop
being sick
to search for sex
to find a mate
all the animals must feel
the same as me

26

Today I got
the nastiest bus driver
in the world
for some weird reason

he stopped for me
but gave me his
signature scowl as
I tossed my six quarters
in the till
usually he tries to
sneak by the stop
concealed by
a South Ferry bus
but not today --

he has often breezed
right by me
as I tried to wave him
down and he has
speeded up when he saw
me running through
traffic across Allen Street
and has left me gasping
exhaust fumes in disgust

he hates to open
the door for passengers
to get on or off
it's against his principals
he also likes to
purposely not stop
when you have reached
your most convenient
destination --
instead of dumping me
at Duane Street
near the Federal Building
closing the door
and stepping on the gas
before I can
quite get my foot
off the last step,

he shoots on
through the tunnel
and sets me down
in City Hall Park
among the pigeons
at the last stop
not one but two stops
past the one I need
he usually runs
a couple lights on the way
and guns the bus for fun

oh boy, here comes
my stop
maybe this is my lucky
day -- after all,
he did let me
get on

27

More garbage trucks
than usual are out on
the streets
making me speculate
that Thursday
must be garbage day
around here

the independent trucks,
which you can tell
by the sodden giant
teddy bear
attached to the
front grill,
are manned by would be
or actual gangsters

who feel no loyalty
whatsoever to the
New York State rules
of the road

one of their missions
in addition to making a disgusting
mess of the trash can storage areas
by trailing banana peels
kitty litter and chicken bones
mixed with moldy coffee grinds
to the rear compactor
is to run pedestrians
down like dogs

I believe they get some kind
of award for this

Anyway -- they are out
in force today
bombing around corners
and through caution lights
at full speed
so I will watch my step
even though this poetic
commentary
may send me on
a little trip to the
bottom of the East River
wearing some very heavy
shoes

28

My mind is
burning now
with anger

I missed my bus
I could have made it
by running if the
Mystic Oil truck
had not been blocking
the entire stop
I prayed that it
was about to pull out
but the oil guy was
just starting his
annoying routine
turned that fuel oil carrier
on full blast
its huge grinding motor
drowning out
my calm morning

all the other drivers
drove past the oil truck
to exit and pick up passengers
but the City Hall bus
after seeing me run to the
front end of the still
rumbling Mystic Oil truck
stopped at the rear of it
with a destination
sign so dirty I couldn't really
be sure I was getting on
the right one
"City Hall?" I barked at
the driver who nodded
almost imperceptibly
with his smirky face
I slammed my token in the slot
and slammed myself
into the only available seat
by the time we arrive
at the Federal Building

I have ignited
in a ball
of furious
flames.

29

It should be warm by now
but I feel like I have been
too long in the freezer
chopping ice from the walls
the sun is bright
clear like summer when there
is no pollution
The bus is a squeaky one today
without my medication
I would be able to hear
what the emergency exit window
is trying to tell me
but now it is just a screeching creak
my ear always totally tuned in
to all such annoyances
the bus is otherwise anonymous
and unobtrusive
all the passengers are in a trance
except one small baby
who doesn't know better
the shadows of skeleton trees
on the gas station marquee
seem weird without the leaves
this winter elongation
makes me feel like we
have been tossed
into another dimension
where the stage props--
-this bus
-that crying singing baby

-the multitude of trucks
 bustling in early morning Chinatown
appear the same
as the ones engraved in my brain
but in this new reality
everything will always be cold
will always move slow
will always chatter its teeth
and creak its bus windows
relentlessly

30

It's another bad
miserable disgusting
uncomfortable deluging
wet as a dog
day
I am that dog
I am wet
the bus windows
are all steamed up
with morning breath
of passengers

the bus dispatcher
took pity
made my bus wait
for me

I am thinking about garbage
being washed away
about winter being melted
I try not to focus on
clammy pant legs
or dripping knapsack

or other riders
on this crowded bus who are
looking over my shoulder
as I scribble
I am late again
no longer able to get
in step with daylight savings
my body no longer flexible
enough or
my mind accepting of
adjustments
to this already invented
artificial reality

It will rain like this all day
I will be inside for most of it
watching the scenery getting
drowned on Church Street
in lower Manhattan
from my office window
my plants will be dreaming
of sticking their roots into
the ground again
and bursting into new growth
I don't have the heart
to tell them
it's not like that anymore
no real dirt in this fair city
only fumes
and toxic mud

they are better off
on the windowsill
with their green
delusions

Couldn't even find
my pen
it's one of THOSE mornings
I'm late enough
so the backs of all
the trucks are open
men toss boxes and crates
dollies and forklifts
maneuver the street
filled with wontons,
fresh vegetables,
red mesh bags of onions
various packages of
items prearranged and
shrink-wrapped
in plastic to fit the
forklift tines

the bus dispatcher
used to like me
and once timidly squeezed out
a cheerful morning greeting
to which I croaked
an asthmatic grudging response
but I am not a social creature

in the morning
I am fresh from
nightly grappling
with unremembered
and unsettling dreams
that in the past I have
recalled enough of
to realize that I have
been engaged

in mortal combat with
gruesome demons and foes
for the last six hours
because of this I think of
the bus dispatcher as
just another potential
danger
another adversary
to be dealt with
by refusing to
acknowledge
his existence

32

More sullen than
usual I look at
my watch
needlessly
because my mind
is not warmed up
enough to
comprehend the time
just so I don't
have to say hello
to the bus dispatcher
who is alone
at the stop
this morning
his predecessor
a man older
than him and
definitely from
the glory days
of Brooklyn
should have warned

him about me
should have done
a bus stop evaluation
including brief notes
on the most
annoying prospective
bus passengers
I would have been
passenger X
the one who snarls
with every move
the impolite
one with
all the wrinkles
around her mouth
from an overdose
of frowning
then he would
know better than
to expect me
to be human
I am like a coiled
snake slithering
around the MTA
bus sign pole
I am like a
swarm of killer bees
I go to way too
much trouble to
avoid all contact
with my peers
it's only common
decency to say
good morning
but it is not
a good morning
I forgot to take
my insulin

and there will
be hell to
pay

33

I awoke bathed in
a cool fresh breeze
the weatherman guaranteed
things will warm up today
everyone is hopeful
in their light jackets
too light for this morning
chill morning air
the gray panthers on this bus
know better
dressing light too soon
can lead to serious illness
just ask anybody's mother
they are bundled up to
the neck in fur coats
but will sweat this afternoon
sweat is good for you
cools the warm body
glistens on the
exercised skin
the bus stops in front
of the Lobster Farm near
Division Street
I love the street names
in this city
like Charlie Parker Square
in the East Village

I imagine him so clearly
nodding out in a
dark room overlooking

the street that now bears
his name
the movie about him
doesn't show the park
it is more concerned with
the revelation of
Parker's horrible problems --
of how he can't live with
the idea of a helpless
damaged daughter
or really live
with the idea of anything
at all
If these defects
are some of the
criteria --
along with having a great
talent that never pans
out the way it should --
then I stand a good
chance of someday
having a street
or alley maybe --
named after me.

34

The second nice day
of spring has begun
of course my body is
wracked with various pains
but at least
they are not complicated
by outrageous
weather offensives

Everyone is sporting
light breezy jackets
I am in black suede
I don't own a
springtime jacket
although I have maybe
ten leather ones
they are too punk
for work with spikes
and band buttons and
paintings on them

this day reminds me in
its feel of a day
I sat on a wrought iron
fence on Park Avenue South
hung over in
the early afternoon
smoking bummed cigarettes
waiting for
my Italian boyfriend
to return from stealing
fancy art books at high class
stores that we would sell
at the Strand to get cash
for dope and coke
I did not actually do any
stealing myself that time
but I encouraged it
I wanted to feed my habit

this bus ride is smooth
and tugs me gently away
from rough memories
I will not take much
of a chance with my life
today
I will ride

a few more blocks
and go be
normal

35

A young boy
passes me
maybe a teenager
but just barely,
tall and tough looking
he cradles his radio
like it was a baby
his fingers caress
the control dials
and buttons

today traffic will be
excellent
the mayor is cracking down
zero tolerance
he calls it
bad parkers
signal failures
red light runners
will be ticketed
I step over glassine bags
on my stoop
and see the sidewalk
clotted with erotic phone sex
advertisements
in every bright color --
if the risqué model
wasn't so visible on them
these cards could have been
construction paper cut up
by a child

the children also step over
glassine bags and sex invitations
on their way to school

The Long Island Expressway
closed lanes this morning
causing great delays
a downed motorcycle
the helicopter traffic guy
said
it will take
a long time to
clear this one
he announces cheerfully
I can picture the scene
I saw the remains of a bike
accident once
two crumpled twisted lumps
of metal
and two empty helmets
side by side
in the road
I wonder if I know
the rider

Last night
40,000 stuck in the subway
from an explosion
I ponder all this
from my relatively safe
seat on the downtown
bus

36

The small trees
in the park

are completely green
the large ones
need more time
I can still see their
winter adornments
plastic bags,
streamers of audio tape
and other forms of
decorative garbage
that have landed in their
branches
out of reach of the
Department of Sanitation

a garbage truck -- a sweeper,
the one with the two huge
rotating brushes
and water sprayers
that sanitation engineers
like to call a "broom" -- whirled
around my corner on Houston
like a giant PacMan
cutting the curb so close
it almost knocked me down
however, I had to admire
the garbage truck driver
because he didn't hit me and
obviously had
pin point control
every morning now
I feel safer bumping
and jiggling in my bus
out of the reach of most traffic
Everyone is silent
this vehicle
could be a tomb
we are too appalled to speak
on this gorgeous

fresh clear sun drenched day
horrorstricken with
the idea that we
are on our way to
work

37

Skywriters have been up
at dawn
already there are
puffy trails
of vanishing messages
across the blue gray
masquerade of heaven
above Allen Street
on radiant display for
my enjoyment

I have a friend who is
sick of life
there is no hope for him
he says
glowering his stoned-out
eyes in my direction
yesterday

I am just starting out
as I hit middle age
I have never even
been in love
I don't want to die
before I feel the hearts
and flowers of romance
bloody hearts and dead flowers
would be best in my case
but nevertheless

it would still be
romance
so I plan to stick around
and continue
my endless searching

my friend has asked
for help
but when given
he accepts nothing
he will do whatever
the drink desires him to
but I need all the help
that I can get
I usually don't ask
until it is almost too late
but always get it anyway

I have said my prayer for him,
my friend,
and will move on
the choice is mine
I can not be his savior
I only hope that
I am strong enough
to save myself

The bus is coming now
I notice that
the messages in the sky
are completely gone

solid gray sky above
with a few slight

patches of light -- hides
the glow that is still
there behind
all this bland atmosphere

The bus driver turns on
the windshield wipers to
scrape away at
the front window

I feel lucky
passengers are stacked up
at every stop and I
waited only 2 minutes

I am all depressed
as I am every morning
after listening to
horrible stories of
child abuse and murder
just so I can
hear the weather
on News Radio 88

the rot was always there
I know but
it seems like there has
been a recent escalation
like one sad beating murder
has unleashed this city's
defective parents until
they fall like dominoes
in a contest to see
who can sink to
the lowest rung of depravity
of hell
this world is full
of pain enough

without being born
into a
crumbling foundation
to a family of parental
sociopaths
to become a prop
to someone's rampant insanity
just a like rag doll
and not a human
and soon just another sad
memory

the sky is still gray
and the motion of
the windshield wipers
makes me feel
like crying

39

Heavy fog
hangs down
thick with spray
refreshing me
rains have washed
the sidewalks and
NYC is clean
the delivery trucks are
triple parked
cutting off two lanes
on Allen Street
at 7:05 AM
the streets crawl
with vague beings
moving through the
gray shrouded air

I am chilled to the bone
with its wetness
but I like it
it is Manhattan as it
really is -- an island
surrounded by water
which has finally taken
over the controls
Do Not Adjust
this is the truth and
happens only
one day a year
so enjoy it

40

If I am not joyful today
I am at least content
my parrots are
fed and watered
they will have a good time
cracking open seeds
and sleeping while
I am grinding away at work
the strong sun has
blasted my brain
into a bad headache and
I remember why I
usually ride the bus
so early
it's 8:00 AM -- all
the other people are out
and that blistering orb
has risen over Brooklyn
in the East
that's where the sun rises

so I must be facing England
as I stand at the M-15
bus stop and someone
over in England
is probably facing me
waiting for their
morning ride
we are facing each other
and everyone is facing
everyone else
we will never meet
and if we met
we would never know that
we had once
faced each other from across
the world while some
higher power
was looking down
at this, knowing
what was happening
considering the whole
incident
of facing each other
a significant event
maybe even arranging it
that way
and it is important
as I move slightly
to ease my painful waiting feet
and disturb a bunch
of molecules
that sets off a chain reaction
or is simply a part
of one already in progress
from the beginning
of existence and
that will never end

This is the PM bus
the after 4:30 can't believe
it's all over bus
the payday bus
where I am heading home
after spending inordinate
amounts on computer
software
on CD ROMS
all probably worth
no more than
$2.50
This is the PM bus
it must be following
right on the tail
of the previous uptown
M-15 from City Hall
they like to travel in packs
and no one got on
at the courthouse
only one new rider at
the DMV
the PM bus
with no suspension
feels as if its belly
is scraping along
Worth Street
and is engaging
every pothole in a
close encounter of
the bus kind
jarring my bones
riding the PM bus
we are in Chinatown
always so much more

exotic in the evening
when most of the produce
and fish trucks have gone
and the fruits shine
in geometric layers in
the fruit stands
I can see the crabs
wiggling in their
white plastic buckets
I'm not sure if turtles
are still sold here
for soup
the shadows are long
the sun could be a summer sun
but it is still very cold
It is the first of May --
May Day
May Day May Day
I am alone
me and my expensive software
heading home
to my parrots and my computer
May Day May Day
I am alone
on the PM bus

42

There may be
hope for us yet
the day is beautiful
this spring feels like fall
I'm not complaining
fall is my favorite
season

My body still isn't
happy with the change
to daylight savings time
I think it ridiculous that
I continue to be off balance
but my shrink says
some people never adjust
That is definitely me --
some people
because I seem to be
affected differently
pills that calm most wake
me up and send me
into fits of wild dervishing
pills for weight loss
increase my appetite
make me gain
consuming sugar by
the ton makes me lose
I am a diabetic
all bets are off
all acceptable behaviors
all responses are
iffy

At this hour -- 8 AM --
still before my official
reporting time -- but later
than usual for me --
all the school children
are reluctantly trudging
toward their higher learning
institution
with long bulky jeans
or khakis
the rear ends of which
are slung down so low
the ass of the pants

nearly drags on the ground
their sneaker strings are untied
the flap is out and flapping
as it should be, I suppose
they wear backwards and forwards
baseball caps and knapsacks
of outrageous colors
they are sending their message
identifying themselves
making their marks
as the "Draggy Pants
Generation"
I do not criticize
only observize
I still wear my spikes
and leather and death black
and chains whenever I
get the chance
I who am covered with
hidden tattoos
do not criticize
and I love the bus driver
on the South Ferry line
who wears a studded dog collar
around his neck
to wild eyed stares of
normal passengers
there are a lot of us
who have not forgotten
our searches for identity
and some who are
still searching including me
that's why I can not
criticize the draggy pants
flapping flaps generation
as I watch them moving
through the fog of life
on this dreary morning

43

It's raining
last night there was
an earthquake in
Seattle
Yesterday was one
of the top ten days
of the year but yesterday
is gone
Bus wipers going
tranquilizing
repetition of sound
that calms me

this is the last day
that I can be late
all these people
on the late buses
are too much for me
and today I am
the latest I have been
yet
my head is wrapped
in rubber bands
the bus driver
has a pony tail and
looks about eighteen
but her driving
is smooth
they gave her a decent bus
with half a suspension
good brakes
her head is barely
visible
above the high-backed

driver's chair
but she rides us
like a soft dream

between the smoothness
and the wipers
I am getting drowsy
think about staying
on until the last stop
at Park Row
and taking the return
bus home
but there is work to do
meetings to be conducted
manuals to be written
paper to be pushed
and so
I yawn at the thought
and get off
at my usual
stop

44

I feel thin
the bus passes
Rivington
I like this feeling
the bus crosses
Delancey
insulin mixes with
my tissues
it will make me
hungry
I have to ignore it
I have my choice of
hungers

the barbed wire
or razor wire as
it is now called
adorns a construction
barrier on Hester
I am being carried
toward my day
where I will
deal with people
who will make me
miserable
and I will get hungry
I will need soothing
we go under
the exit ramp for
the Brooklyn Bridge

the Chinese fish stands
are empty
the fish displays
are filled with ice
that is clean
and looks like snow

my body is an anarchist
I am plotting
how to bring it into line
without convening
a firing squad

Worth Street appears
under the neon sign
for Dr. Toothy the dentist
everything is
fresh and beautiful
the Chinese ladies

exercise gracefully
in the park
the line for
Motor Vehicles
is forming
I wonder with my
mental backdrop
the bus driver's
basketball discussion
if I will make it
through this day

45

Too much sun
I duck away from it
trying to reposition
myself
at the bus stop
to avoid its rays
to avoid getting a
headache from squinting

the bus dispatcher
is looking at me funny
I must seem
like a morning vampire
I have on sunglasses
and almost always do
to protect my sensitive
blues or some say grays
I would like a gigantic pair
of sunglasses to cover
the ones I am already wearing
to stop the sun
from driving its

stake in my heart
in my brain

The Methodonians
don't look happy to
be in the revealing brightness
I must get up earlier tomorrow

I feel better
we have turned the big
corner near the
Chinatown monument where
a man shimmers by in a sharkskin suit
and we are finally driving away
from the sun

I wonder how I will feel
when summer comes

46

The more I say I
will come
early the later
I go
this bus is too crowded
to write until
we reach the
far eastern edge of
Chinatown
and so instead
I thought about
Nero the Parrot
who has started flying
to me from
across the room

he is trying to be
the pet I always
said I wanted
and he tries to
play with me
and be my little
parrot boy
I want to crush him
I restrain myself
the same way I
always have to do
with people

47

Nerves are falling over
the edge
the city continues its run
of bad weather
with a cold wet chiller
and a gray soggy blanket
over all of it
fat precipitation begins
the second
I exit my front door

late I am late
the morning at home
is so enticing
conducting detailed searches
for lost things
I want to stay there
and look some more

fuck this day

which has already begun
to ache in my back
already sending waves of misery
to catch up with me
in the crowded bus
where I must contort
my writing style
because knowing someone
can see ruins everything
I bend my notebook
and write almost
upside-down
I am quite sure
they have seen me
trying to hide
only making them more interested
pulling them
to crane their necks
until the whole section
of blatant watchers
around me
all get up and exit at
the same stop

I am already deep
into today's paranoia
fear and hatred
so they might as well
have kept on looking
but if I was them
I would be enjoying
the view out the
bus window
no longer doomed to
this frenzied scribbling

On the bus
zooming
after intaking
heart rumbling noises
of trucks
some days my ears
are sensitive to noise
everything I hear seems like
noise
other days the same
sounds are music

the industrial bus waiting song
the ten ton truck song
as their motors blast
and their size causes
the sidewalk to shake
I wonder how solid
the ground is that
we are all standing on
here in NYC
it has not yet cracked
and swallowed us up --
but I am sure it will

I wish my friend Charlene
got on at my stop
she would talk to
the people and
draw me into their lives
she would be a conduit
for this reclusive
atomic particle
I would know everyone
the bus dispatcher would be

happier
all the people I've been
riding with for years
would be happier
even if we are not standing
on solid ground
even if the grating rusted
noise/music trucks
remind us with their
expositions of surface
instability
we will all be happier
to be here
at the bus stop
at 8:15 AM
Friday morning --

49

In the beautiful
clear atmosphere
sparking sunlight
cloudless sky
I am late for work
again
I am close to setting
an all time record
but this is actually good
because in the past
these late for work days
would have been
no work at all days
which although relaxing
at the time eventually
results in
massive anxiety

the park benches
are empty
it was cold last night
and homeless plastic
cardboard campers
may have moved indoors
or else the mayor has been
on the move again
cleaning up the quality
of some lives
by destroying others

thoughts like this do
not fit the gorgeous sunlight
it seems that no one
could be suffering today
but we all know
that's not true

if we didn't suffer they say,
there would be no joy --
funny, sometimes I would
settle for a level
plateau of emotions
to do away with pain

out the bus window
an Asian mother
wipes tears from her
boy's face
in the front seat of
a car below that
I am looking
down on
a man is driving,
the boy is on her lap
sobbing

I wonder if the boy
is sick
or if his father
has recently smashed
him in the head

50

Dappled sun across
dilapidated
tenement buildings
romanticizes them
the occasional vacant lot
reminds me of
my red dog Hymie
who was killed
crossing 2nd Avenue
in 1968 and was buried
in a vacant lot by
my friend who found his
broken body in the gutter

where I left him
not having the heart
required to do it myself
and not wanting
to give him over to
the sanitation department
Hymie rests beneath
Lower East Side rubble
and I have never really
moved forward since
the day he died.
On the bus,
I hate the other passengers
and I hate myself

but I don't hate the sunlight
which today is beauty
and purification
streaking across
everything so brightly
sparkling on car windows
revealing the true greenness
of the trees
making everyone wear
sunglasses and appear mysterious
lighting our way forward
into destiny

51

8:30 AM
promising day ahead
weather wise at least
the bus is not crowded although
my favorite single seats
that run along
the left side
are all taken
I am not unique
everybody wants them
wants to sit alone and
ride in peace

I wonder what
The Village Voice
has against me
The fourth time now
they have not listed
my upcoming show
It's pointless to speculate
most likely
they don't know me

from a hole in the ground
and have omitted
my listing
from sheer ignorance

the orange bags of onions
look elegant
highlighted by sun streaks
the onions are big and round
promising to lend their flavor
to the universe
the bus command center
breaks in
to announce the time
8:37 AM as we make our
turn onto East Broadway
it's slower to come
in late to work
the huge supermarket delivery
trucks and hordes of school children
clog up the streets
but we have
made a breakaway and
glide to Chatham Square
without catching one traffic light

my eyebrow is hinting
that it will
begin to twitch again
set in motion three weeks ago
by a poet's scream
Worth Street appears
on the horizon
its time to ring the bell
and get off
join my daily battle
with stronger paper
enemies

52

Thursday in the rain
slight drizzle now
I am dressed for it
people cough on the bus
I have a scratchy throat
hint of an earache
the bus driver honks and says
"Oh please" as a
white kid starts to cross
the instant the traffic
light flashes its
"Don't Walk" warning
some sidewalkers have
opened their umbrellas
others don't bother
depending on their
raindrop and one hand
in the air
tolerance levels
I am low on both
homeless types hawk newspapers
to car windows and one
gives our driver
a Daily News for free
which I believe
is the same price
he got it for
ordinarily he gets a quarter
he says hopefully
The driver just says "thank you"
I haven't read a paper
in so long, I can't recall the
regular price
I get all the bad news

I can handle without
asking for more

I leave the papers at
the newsstand even though
they do print the
daily and weekly lotto numbers
and I always have to get
them from a chart at
the lottery ticket sellers' store
but this inconvenience
I can tolerate
to avoid the incessant
headlines touting war
murder child abuse
dismembering strangulation
political low jinx
global unrest and upheaval
I know its happening
I don't require daily
misery updates
I want to hear about
some good things
to feel some happy emotions
the things that make
living endurable
the news that no one writes about
that is rarely found

at least, I think there may
be something good happening
somewhere
but I will not hear
about it this
Thursday
in the rain

I have made a good
start today
bouncing down
Allen Street before 7:30 AM
I forgot my watch
but I recognize
all my early morning
riding companions
like the guy with
Brillo Pad hair who
shaved himself bald
last summer
and the tiny black man
with the twisted body
and tiny cane
who always wears
a beret and headphones
to complete his ensemble

Everyone has shiny shoes
even me
a black man who looks
like a jazz guy
sports penny loafers
with tassels
they gleam
the heavy guy who usually
has on a suit must be doing
Dress Down Friday
in khakis and casual jacket
he has on huge black
formal shoes also shining
my high-heeled shoes
of dull tanned leather
are shining too
they have been freshly polished

and will retain this sheen
for just about as long
as it takes me to walk
the three blocks to work
from the bus stop
the lady with neatly coifed
red hair tries to
dump her used paper
on the driver
who refuses this smudged gift
the lady always reads the
NY Times
looks real snooty -- too
perfect to be real
her off-white shoes
glisten, distracting attention
from her thick legs
she treats all
the drivers kindly
unlike myself
who only sits and writes

54

I saw a bird disintegrate
this week
yesterday I first noticed it
already mangled
just a beautiful unsquashed
wing with brown and
yellow markings
and a small yellow beak
protruded from its
tiny wreck
as we rolled our
hand truck over the wing tip
on our way home to

Clinton Street

I said to Jan:
"You just ran over a
baby bird"
she groaned:
"Did you have to tell me?"

Her small remark
brought an avalanche
of guilt descending
as I remembered
those who told me
things I didn't need to know,
like my boyfriend Robert
who once looked at some
photographs and chirped at me:
"Boy, you look really fat in these,"
or other times when he
would advise: "That poem needs
a lot of editing," or:
"It was better the other way,"
this critique came mostly
after I had read the poem
in question to wild
applause at the same reading
where his own poem had settled
down into well-deserved
leaden obscurity without
comment from me
like when I left my second
husband and my mother wrote
how cruel I was and how it
was good I didn't have a
child because I would probably
decide to get rid of it too,
and how I cried for Theo

JD Rage and Jan Schmidt, co-founders of Venom Press
photo by Arthur Rivers

JD Rage and Jan Schmidt, co-founders of Venom Press
photo by Arthur Rivers

then and the other two
whose arrivals in this world
have been indefinitely
delayed
my baby boy, who if
now alive will be a man
a disintegrating memory

his adult appearance
unknown to me
not even a brown and yellow
wing to capture him
I saw the bird's remains again
today and if I hadn't noticed
yesterday I would not
have been able to tell
what that lumpy brown spot
on the sidewalk was

55

we will break the heat
record again
two days in a row before
this year's Memorial celebration
I hope this doesn't mean that
summer will be an unbearable
oven with blackouts
unexpected deaths
and fried brains

I fried my own brain
in a summer heat wave
deep in a boiling subway pit
I could feel my head swelling
in that blistering
underground furnace

I have not recovered yet
from that experience
I almost wound up back
in the bottle again
had I not refrained from
drink, I would have
been seen yesterday,
stumbling up
the middle of Avenue A
in 96 degrees, one arm
draped around my ragged
booze-soaked pal
together we would have been
crooning:
Puff The Magic Dragon
Lived By The Sea.....

56

Last night a cop was killed
by a broken mirror
blood gush from
a slashed thigh
an incident that could
not be controlled
after he fell on it

this bus is a broken mirror
all our lives reflected in
the jagged shards

this city is a broken mirror
the mayor is selling off
all the basic services
(the ones he is not simply
canceling)

like the water system
and the transit authority
I want to know who
would buy them

Who would purchase
this rundown vehicle
certainly a shining chariot
when compared to the
average subway car?

Bright green bags are
being unloaded from the trucks
I can't tell what's inside
one vampire passenger
has sucked blood from
the bus dispatcher
who is not our usual man
but a tall mean-looking one
who entrances me--
now the demon
hovers over a
female passenger
just opposite from my seat
as we roar off from
the stop where the
now pale dispatcher
gingerly holds his throat

she talks and touches
respectfully but too obviously
and too often
I know she is a vampire
I see her in a sliver of
the broken mirror
she throws out a reflection
but it is that of a
cardboard doll

she will soon be sucking out
more than pleasant conversation

I must be very careful on this bus
before I lose my neck

57

The mean bus driver
discusses business with
the dispatcher
who has developed,
without my noticing,
a diabolic look
enhanced by
slash of sideburns
and sharp goatee
The driver says he doesn't
get off until 5:30
and it's only 7:30 AM now
maybe that is why he
acts so mean

His pink undershirt sleeves
are longer than the
light blue MTA uniform
he drives with one hand
and makes a lot
of quick turns and screeching
halts

the air is clear and cool
The methadone clinic
has a long waiting line
the driver waves to other
drivers and traffic cops

and crossing guards

A crossing guard was
arrested yesterday
while escorting kiddies
across the street to school
she was a heroin dealer
the brand she sold called
"Now & Yesterday" after
a favorite name
of children's candy

she had bags of heroin on her
when apprehended
and needle tracks along
both arms

On TV horrified parents
were interviewed by the
evening news
parents, of which at least
two, appeared to my studied
eye to be heroin users
themselves

58

On my way to the bus
I saw a 2 of Clubs
on the sidewalk
those playing cards
on the street flash up
at me and used to
all the time
but never one as esoteric
as the 2 of Clubs
never one as indecipherable

as the 2 of Clubs

The Ace of Spades
would turn up frequently
the Queen of Hearts
The King with the ax
the one-eyed Jack
cards fraught with
possible interpretations
to fit the variable
circumstances of anyone's
life

When the bus and I and all
the other passengers
make the big turn
at Chatham Square,
the command center
announcement comes on
with evil-sounding
laughter happening
behind the speaker
who propagandizes us
with the virtues of the
metrocard
and advises it is 7:05 AM
interrupting all my
wondering about the
2 of Clubs
2 what?
What club?
Have I no future
2 minutes to live
am I getting mugged
today?

and as if that is not
enough, there are

exactly 3 branches
broken off the freshly
planted Cherry trees
outside the new
Federal Building
on Duane Street
and another
dead baby bird
with beak open as if
waiting for a worm
on the sidewalk,
near Blimpie's
on Reade Street

59

Woke up feeling great
but somehow pulled a strategic
muscle in my neck
before getting out the front door
probably happened
while I was pulling on
my socks
I will be uncomfortable all day
in this bus seat
in my leather office chair
in the Chinese fast-food at lunch
I am always uncomfortable
anyway
it is life's plan for me
but I don't need any
unnecessary physical
complications

the day itself is a beauty
the bus is empty

although I am late and
it should be packed
the sun is blazing
the air is cool
everything looks clean
in this purifying lighting scheme

the driver shoots up the shortcut
alley near the Mobil Station on
Pike Street
that way he doesn't have to wait
for the traffic light on
East Broadway
he's probably on his way
to breakfast at the end of
the line and the shortcut will
shave at least 2 seconds
off his driving time

my neck shows no sign
of loosening up
the human body is a strange thing
when I finally gave up on
being the most outraged
philosophical mental rebel
I could conjure, resigning only
due to pure exhaustion
my body took over where
my mind left off
and went into absolute revolt
It is completely haywire
and by all rights should be
locked up with no exit key
but it is allowed to walk the streets
unsupervised
and while it rides these buses
I know it spends a lot of time
plotting further ingenious

ways to bring about
my untimely miserable
totally unglamorous
demise

60

Medication fuzzzzz controls
my brain
yet my neck still hurts
through the mask of pharmaceuticals
it is a bad one
I can't remember what I did
to cause such deep contortion
wish that I was home
in bed
but I am on the bus
with another female driver
there are so many of them
one can be quite sure
the bus driver position
is one where the MTA
is not discriminating

a passenger yells
SORRY, after causing
the driver to pull in at an empty stop
she wanted the next one
isn't that always the way it is
now we have passed that one too
she and her sorrow have departed
have debussed

the sun is casting its beauty
all around again
reminding me of cool mornings
in the south topped off

by oven-like afternoons
and a daily rainstorm at 3:30 PM

I will be in my office today
until it cools again
the heat will not affect me
almost like the afternoon weather
isn't going to happen at all

61

wet island chill in the air
I surprise myself by saying
good morning
to the driver
I am not infused with goodwill
but am tired of death
pain and animosity

the sky is gray
made grayer by my viewing it
through dark glasses
but otherwise, I don't see
how I could stand it

the rushing black clouds
are building
bringing rough weather
from the south
it is too depressing
the sky and the bus
and Allen Street with its empty
waiting produce pallets
its red signs with yellow
lettering in Chinese
yes, even the signs in their
artificial brightness

are most depressing
yesterday was the weekend
and Sunday turned out
to be a day
filled with my tears
I cried for dead friends
I cried for the possibility of
humanity that I have never
quite managed to achieve
I cried because I was not dead
and yet through my tears
and under my tears I could feel
someone waiting to be released

62

Just missed the bus in the
pack of three that comes at 7:09
but the 7:20 is fine,
only 5 passengers
and a happy driver with
a big smile
I needed a big smile
after yesterday's
tropical rainstorm from noon
to midnight
today this city is clean

after one minute
the bus reaches the Mobil Station
and we have caught up with the
South Ferry bus near the
Bridal Wedding Studio
at Catherine Street
There is very little traffic
we will have more rain

we will all be clean
we will grow
the bus breezes past the
Asian exercisers
all men today
in yellow polyester alligator shirts
jabbing and thrusting
One person is already in line at
the DMV for a road test
or learner's permit
or license plate
At 7:26 we turn off Worth
I am here

time to stop scribbling and
get real

63

It's already a bad day
at 7:25 AM
I passed two young starlings
drinking from a puddle
and they made me smile
which is quite a trick
at this hour
but then the smokers
made their appearance
insisting on passing me
so I could breathe in their
exhaled vapor and the
trailing smoke of their
cigarettes that never
enters their lungs,
only mine --
I take much longer to get

to the bus stop
dropping back to avoid
this portable pollution
and spending the rest
of my day in a wheezing funk

When I crossed Allen Street
on the green
the South Ferry bus 8191
cut the corner so close
it seemed done on purpose
with malicious intent
my back went into spasm
my neck was already screwed up
and got worse
when I jumped onto the sidewalk

At the stop
I was alone
which meant those smokers
probably caused me to miss
my bus to City Hall
then the stop began
to fill with all the most
grotesque passengers
the ones it's hard to look at
the ones who relentlessly
remain in my head after I see them
the ones I always get stuck riding with
two inches from my nose
in the elevator at work
who sing opera at the top of their lungs
who burst out spontaneously
with Tourettes Syndrome obscenities
who drool, and talk nonsense
yes, they all converged on me
at once

To avoid their influence
I gazed uptown
and saw a humid mist enveloping
First Avenue
A solid curtain that if
I were looking downtown from there
I would see myself enshrouded in

The bus came
I got on
and melted into the lovely
air conditioning
with only one of these wackos
directly in my line of sight
because, fortunately
I couldn't see myself.

64

I got the cheerful driver
again today
I guess my mind is getting
back on schedule
if I have managed to make
the same bus two days
in a row
he is not so happy now
but is still dispensing
friendly greetings
to the sullen lot of us
with our hair still wet from
the shower
bags of breakfast coffee
and half-open sleepy eyes

a one-legged bathtub

filled with garbage
has been parked at the bus stop
sometime since yesterday morning
as we head downtown, I see
strange white objects
and split plastic bags displaying
their rotting insides
piled along the sidewalks
a hi-lo adorned with a paisley
stuffed elephant
rolls in and out of view
between two trucks
adjusting itself for the morning
loads of wooden pallets

we almost squash an errant car
near Tong's Realty
then follow a green industrial
uniform delivery van that veers around
corners so fast it seems
that gravity must pull
its occupants out of
the open front door

The trees are fully dressed in green
the exercisers make wide circles
with their arms
we hurl to a stop,
first one of the trip,
at the Department of Health
on Worth Street
mine is next but I am not ready
I want to ride
and ride and ride
and never get off

the new driver's cheery demeanor
has finally faded
today I say hello
he doesn't answer

It's Friday morning
if I am lucky, if I live
through the day,
the weekend will come

the Central Park victim
has been identified
she has three fractures and
is in bad shape
in a coma
she was found in pools
of blood by a dog walker
no one else offered to help
screams went unanswered
everyone saw him
his picture is all over the media
but she doesn't know
what hit her yet
they say she might have
been a music teacher

Allen Street has a sign
that says "Orchard Street - NY
Bargain District"
but it is not Orchard Street,
it is Allen Street and there is not
a bargain in sight
tourists might be confused by this

The radio announcer says
the Central Park Mugger/Assaulter/

Batterer might be a tourist
might be from out of town
because not one of
eight and one half million residents
has turned him in
it's amazing the cops
are so confident that they
have a handle on each one of us
and we can all be eliminated
as suspects

Witnesses saw an argument
she might have been his girlfriend
because usually a batterer
is well known
to the victim
close to the victim
intimate with the victim

I wonder
how much more intimate can
you get than melding
your fist into someone's face
or denting a pipe into their skull
but I am on the bus
the victim is in the hospital
the bus driver is not smiling
and the perpetrating bastard
is running free

66

The air is thick with oxygen particles
and pollution the size and weight
of bowling balls
my hair is wet although I didn't shower
and it isn't raining

I have never seen a year that slapped
us down with such consistently
miserable weather

the bus is nicer than nature
with its thoughtful climate control
devices which for once are working

out the window I see the storefront
for Asian Americans for Equality
there is no other traffic
it is 7:05 AM
the World Trade Center appears
through a crack in the buildings
where East Broadway converges
with Park Row
the top of it is wrapped in a gray
cotton fog
bright pink flowers and pink foam
construction panels dress up the landscape
between the courts and Federal buildings
my ride is over too soon
this morning

67

The sky is Japanese
a painting of dry brush strokes
in different shades of gray

We have the mean driver
who has shaved his head for the summer
which starts in nine days or so
The city is dirty
a sodden mess
its discarded mattresses have become
moldy in the dank air

but since there has been no rain
the streets are filthy
the Sanitation Department can no longer
keep up with us
only nature can sweep us clean
when she feels like it
today she's concentrating on
drowning everyone

My mind is as heavy as the atmosphere
a lead wall
a depression sucking me inward
upon myself
I begin to identify with Dr. Kevorkian's
latest assisted suicide over in New Jersey
whose medical condition as described
on the radio didn't seem much different
from mine

The mean driver rams the M-15 down
Worth Street, stopping for two seconds
to allow some passengers to leap off
At this high speed, I better get ready
now and practice my broad jumping
technique in the aisle
my stop is next and I don't want to
start the day being dragged away
caught in the door of a bus

I believe the friendly dispatcher
has been replaced
it is now ten or more mornings
without him
I no longer dread my approach

to the bus stop
I don't have to think of ways
to avoid the new man

The dispatchers on this route
have all been large tall men
and while there are numerous woman
drivers, I have yet to see
a female dispatcher
it's probably a higher paid job

Last night, the president had a bumpy
ride
I am reminded of this by the jerking
motion of the bus
Air Force One went through a patch
of turbulence
the president was unscathed
but the Secret Service men,
who I imagine that like bus dispatchers
are all men, the presidential
bodyguards were joined in a
food fight with playful air currents
and left the plane covered
in their Mexican dinners

I am going to have a bad day
after three days of weather that
crushes you down before you leave
your door
two more like this to come

Scientists have proved that fat mice
live much shorter lives
but on TV the fat mouse looked cuter
than the lean mean one

The bus dispatcher is fat

I am fat
over half of these passengers are fat
so where does that leave us?
Some of us are not even cute

The saving grace is that there is
probably no bad weather in the
hereafter and there is also the possibility
of an end to suffering

Today's nondescript but slim driver
Makes the inevitable turn on Worth Street
into the home stretch
I wish he could maneuver the bus
to rise up into the sky and then he could
drive it into a nicer day
somewhere else in time

69

I waited a long time for the bus
this morning
when it finally arrived
it was packed to the gills
with more passengers pouring on

gills is a most appropriate comparison
the air is so thick the buses are
swimming downtown
I decided to wait some more
and before the packed M-15 had
moved out of the stop
I had boarded and was under way
on #1659

I got a single seat in the front

and my day will be better for it
Every stop now is filled
with people waiting
until the seats on #1659 are all
taken, but nobody has to stand
We pass a Five Brothers Fat Enterprises
truck, I am surprised by it since
most Chinatown trucks are
covered with graffiti that obliterates
the company names

We engage in a race with another bus
the one behind us passed by
so our driver took the Mobil Station
shortcut and we are once again
the first M-15 in a pack of three
all of us will stop at Catherine Street
the last transfer point for riders
to switch for different destinations
workers arrange oranges, grapefruits
and tomatoes in the stand across
East Broadway
traffic is bad
it's only 8:15
but dark with fog and clouds
and the overwhelming feeling
of wet doom

I notice the dispatchers are all
different today
I think it might be
a changing of the guard
the line of soggy applicants is long
outside the DMV
it still hasn't rained
we've been living in a
communal bathtub these last four days

work, I need to get to work
to my air conditioning and escape
from this disagreeable water world

70

Bus #2242 - mean driver
7:27 AM
a tiny fly lands on me and
dies a horrible death by index
finger squashing
the woman in front of me
is unduly nervous
she turns around when I unzip my bag
to get a nickel and five pennies for my
dollar ten coffee
and jumps in the air when I stretch out my
leg so I could put the change in
my pocket
she turns again when I click
my ballpoint pen
the driver honks
A Wonton Food truck takes the
short cut
we haven't stopped once yet

I must be a suspicious looking type
even in my business suit
the woman is even sitting funny
in her seat to make it easier
for her to turn around and
guard against my imminent attack
well maybe she's right - look what
happened to that poor defenseless fly

The day is gorgeous but still humid
the stink trees are out in all

their stinking splendor
the whole city smells a lot like
underarm BO

71

The bus driver is a jerk
he wouldn't open the doors
until he was the only bus at the stop
ridiculous, because all of us
were ready to get on
he had his little power trip
and then closed the door on
my knapsack
but if he had let us on when
he should have
I wouldn't have been the
last one in

I gave him a look
amazing that he lived through it

Dytrading truck from Jersey
Cuang Jin from Mott Street
are the first things I see
after riding out my anger
L.I.E truck from Brooklyn
LHCO from Monroe Street
Tai Shing from Division
Dai Sing
Names on big white truck
hardly visible through
blue and red graffiti

The passengers are very nervous
jiggling their legs
we pass Sunny Shanghai

noisy garbage grinder
telephone booth ads from NYNEX
and OTB
Wing Fat Shopping Center
I must remember to get my shoes
take a long lunch
pick up a package at the PO
send in my credit card payment
too much to do too much
I would give anything
to exercise on the monkey bars with
the Chinese seniors
to lose this bus
this jerk of a driver and melt

72

I am riding to Newark on
Olympia Trailways
it is a very bumpy ride
I prefer the MTA M-9 bus
that I took from home
to the World Trade Center
It is the muggiest day yet
the air is dripping
rain would be more honest
than this dishrag of particulate
matter imitating a fogged up
bathroom after a hot shower
breathing this into my lungs
I feel that I am drowning
I might never get the chance
to go down over the wilds
of Central New York State
in the continental commuter flight
to Syracuse
the Olympia Driver is copying

10-4ing and standing by
but this bus is moving
tonight I will be sitting around
the barbecue on my brother's deck
hundreds of miles from my home
on Clinton Street
Lower East Side NYC NY USA
North America
The World
The Universe
Boy I will be doing some traveling
today

73

Smoke pours up from an
underground Con Ed worksite
orange signs on the Allen Street Park
median
announce Road Work Ahead
A sign on Delancey warns:
Bump Ahead
Burger King's flag waves
in the morning wind
the Williamsburg Bridge is
hidden by white fog
more smoke
from an orange and white striped
tube topped with dark blue
rises from beneath the pavement
blue and white plastic sheets
undulate on the side of
a decaying tenement
protecting its empty innards
the hi-lo driver communicates
into a walkie talkie
the Mobil Station advertises

friendly serve tire air at
no extra cost
a man with a beret
two men wearing headphones
and two women depart the bus
and two young Asian girls get
on at the last stop on East Broadway
raindrops dot the front windshield
now and umbrellas have gone up
the police cruise up Worth Street
the firearms store is gated up
a man casually crosses
against the light

74

I am glad I do not have to
push myself along in
a maroon wheelchair wearing
a purple baseball cap and
black leather gloves to
protect my hands
right now
but no one can predict the future
ridership is high this Friday
morning
three passengers have boarded
at each stop
that will end since we have
arrived downtown and when
you are already downtown
you don't need to
take the bus to get there

the sullen driver enters
the shortcut lane
and we will undoubtedly be

bumped around and
making abrupt stops
that might throw us all
through the windshield

The weather is horrible
worse is predicted
we round the bend past
the Chinatown OTB
work looms ahead
the biggest cloud on the
horizon

75

didn't want to get up today
pain all over
disfiguring hole in my nose
even when covered by makeup
some diabetic infection bullshit
finally hit the shower
am late but clean
like the sunshine
mottled, bright
not dull like my brain
the bus stop was a cop stop
two of them waited impatiently
and got on the crowded City Hall
that is just in front of the one
I am riding I wanted them to wait
and ride with me, but they are
in a hurry to reach
their destination

We begin racing another bus
side by side down Allen Street
using all the lanes

so the regular traffic
doesn't stand a chance
a truck squeezes by but we have
ended our little competition
the name on the truck door is
Sunbright Corp
somebody's idea of
a cute coincidence

I have on new clothes
but they are already ugly
I worry about my tattoos
my Native American grim reaper
waves a war stick that
extends up high on my
spine and shows
at the base of my neck

more trucks than ever are
parked on East Broadway
a solid line on both sides
all of them are white underneath
most are decorated in
multicolored bilingual graffiti

this side of the bus is hot
near the emergency exit
it's probably where they generate the
air conditioning
basically defeating the purpose

it was an M-9 that we were
racing, we meet up again at
Catherine Street
no one switches
the uptown bus passes by
and has only three riders

they are highlighted
in the bright sun that streaks
across their faces
I see that there are a lot of cops
out today
both Clinton (whose wifey stands
accused of conversing with
Eleanor Roosevelt) and
Pineapple Boy Dole will be
in town performing their number one
function in life - screwing up traffic

76

Delancey Street coming up
announces the driver
as I pant breathlessly
after running like hell
in my new dress to
catch this bus
nearly giving my life
in the process
only one step faster than
the heavy dump truck
who angrily honked his
way around the corner
at those inconsiderate pedestrians
who insisted on crossing
the street on the WALK light
it is almost always better
to go when DON'T WALK
is flashing
in the game of Catch the Bus
after the snorting blasting
madness of traffic is gone
Another absurd facet in the NYC

contest of Live Or Die

Once I am safely on this conveyance
a loudmouth kid screeches and
writhes across the aisle
only his mother is louder
telling him to STOP
all of us sleepers in our private comas
become annoyed
I hope she will get off at
the Methadone Program
so both of them can calm down
but she is not drugged out
and they are straight and pure irritation
delighting in their own cacophony
Noise can be a good thing but not
when it Ya Ya Ya Ya's you at 7:44 AM

When she prepares to get off at my stop
I am surprised when I recognize them
as baby Vance and his working mom
the only reason I know the baby's name
is from her always yelling at him to
WAKE UP when the bus approaches
Duane Street
he usually must arouse himself
from a deep stupor but
today Vance himself yelled
all the way from Houston Street
to Federal Plaza and
now I am ready to join his cry
I guess he must be growing up
and knowing where
he is going.

All the ladies are decked out
in flowery motifs
it is already summer
but cool to start this day
there is no visible soot, fog, smog,
grime or drizzle nor odors of kitty litter,
gaseous sewer returns
or rotting garbage
What is wrong with this picture?
Can all 8 million of us be clean
at the same time?

I guess so, except for the wad
of gum stuck at the base of
my doorway which I thought
was a stray sunflower seed
from Nero's food and picked up
only to stick to the stairway railing
in disgust so I could lock my door before
tossing it well into the incinerator
but that was only the precursor
to the gum I stepped in
just outside my building
half-concealed in the cracked remains
of a plastic coffee cup top
which I could not remove
even after doing those weird
foot scraping contortionist dances
that are not supposed to look like
you are trying to get something
off your foot
but in reality you look like
a horse counting numbers with his
hoof and what could be more
obvious than that
so the air can be fresh

and the day can be glorious
but the bottom of my shoe
tells it like it is.

78

M-9 nighttime bus 8:57 PM
very punctual arrival
but before pulling away
from the stop,
the driver gets out and
checks the front end
he has a plastic gallon jug
of water in his hand
but seems to feel no need
to use it
he reboards and drives us for
a block or two
when the bus began to beep
some kind of warning signal
and now I wonder
when he gets out again and
starts banging on the buses
nose if we will make it
all the way to Avenue B on
this obvious lemon
PA 2601.

I notice warning signs posted
all around me ordering:
Do Not Talk To The Driver
No Littering
No Smoking
No Spitting
No Radio Playing

Oriental passengers come aboard
in Chinatown carrying eight or nine
pink or orange plastic bags apiece
carrying all fresh foods
that may or may not be good for them
last year it was salmonella in
the Caesar salad from undercooked eggs
and in the kitchen sink from unwashed
knives used to cut raw meat
this year it is on the raspberries
and strawberries and possibly
all fresh produce
so beware
those healthy foods may kill you
faster than the hazardous ones
those where all the vitamins and
bacteria are nuked or freeze-dried
or leeched away by chemical additives

Pause: as the bus shuts itself off until
severely tweaked by the driver

So I, with my diet of frozen foods
and sugar-free products, will be alive
(though most likely covered with
huge disfiguring tumors)
while the healthy eaters will be
long dead in their graves or urns
killed by bacteria poisoning
before the long-term benefits of
vitamins can do them any good

The bus is pulling in at Delancey
only a few blocks from my stop
If this bus should die from
over-exertion, cheap motor oil
and dehydration, I can walk home
from here

Actually, I can walk from anywhere
to anywhere else, but for some reason
I am now rounding the corner
on Houston and A
on this wheezing, uncomfortable
better-than-average smelly
NYC bus.

79

The bus and I today apexed
in one fluid motion
it was better than sex - the doors
opened as I reached the sidewalk
by crossing in front of the
monstrous vehicle just in time
without running
a second later
would have spelled disaster

All is right on Allen and Delancey
but all is not well in Saudi Arabia
where a symbolic gesture
aimed at Saudi leaders has cost
the lives of the American troops
who were blown sky high
by a truck bomb
This action taken to demonstrate
that the Americans cannot even
protect themselves.

These troops were the remainder
left to show support
to protect against further acts
of war or terrorism

One American mother
expecting her boy home on furlough
happily ran to get the door
and welcome him found instead
a messenger from the
U.S. Military bring her
the news of his death

and all the papers play the sympathy
angle trying to enrage us reporting
that one dead Air Force guy was
to have married in October his
Air Force fiancée
but the headlines did not mention
their inevitable divorce one or two
years later or the possible spousal
abuse that either of them might
have inflicted on the other
and are now spared from

I am told repeatedly that things
happen exactly as they are supposed to
but on days so near to a tear jerking
tragedy as this one
it is hard to
believe
that
this was the way things
were meant to be

Oh, but we are not to attempt
to unravel this, to figure it out
too much thinking
can lead to disaster
but not much thinking is
required in this situation
to see that no matter how you

look at it
there could have been a
better way.

80

Margo Hemingway is dead
she was an alcoholic
found severely decomposed
only a few days from
her last appearance in public
no foul play is suspected
no evidence of suicide
ha ha

I am in my favorite seat
in the M-15 to City Hall
PA 4315
I am alive
an alcoholic
in an arrested state of decomposition

Today, I am comparing
the things of the city
with the things of a wildlife
sanctuary
Dionondehowa Preserve
that flourishes under the protective
eye of Equinox Mountain

Overhead fly city seagulls
gliding sometimes in a similar way
to the flight of a Turkey Vulture
above the fields of tall grasses
and healing weeds

There are miles of iron fences lining

the concrete park on Allen Street
the trees though green are choked
with constant fumes and will
never feel the brush of a
coyote tail across their trunks

The people are anxious to
get to work
where they will be safe from the
city dangers like the
blackened bum
who yells: "Advanca!!!"
at the snarling traffic
from his bed upon a cardboard mat

he is rotting
much like fallen forest trees
but the cement will not
claim his bones.

81

The city has a background noise
like feedback like the hissing of music
over the headphones
like bus windows vibrating
I have the energy today
like the pigeon I passed
who leapt from the curb
with the strength of a pogo spring

The bus is packed PA679
the eve of the 4th of July
large bombs went off
near Clinton Street last night
while the mayor announced
no fireworks will be sold
this year

not even in Chinatown
not even to mob bosses
somehow I can't envision
the truth of his remark
since two children
have already blown off fingers
and others have burned down a house
in Queens by setting off
M-80's on the roof

Peter Missing used to set off
M-80's at the Limelight
immediately clearing hordes
of dancing lawyers and doctors
from the room
but Peter was old enough to
understand the consequences
of the permanent loss of a limb
a digit an eye or two
leave your pyrotechnics to the experts

The bus is passing through
Chinatown now
home of the firecracker

As I look uptown, I see two men
scurry across the street
foolishly risking their lives
in order to beat out the oncoming
traffic and make it to the other side
massive rumbling trucks whiz by
missing them by less than a hair

the passengers around me are quiet
reading or deep in thought
we are all getting ready for the
everyday explosions
that lie ahead.

The fireworks are over now
I saw the glow as each bomb
went off above the East River
but not reaching high enough
for me to see the colors
from my bedroom
window

it is all part of a mob war
City Hall vs. John Gotti
One gang is sanctioned
the other is in jail
the lowlife citizenry are not allowed
to provide their own
explosives
not allowed to burst their bombs
in midair over NYC

The heavyset dispatcher
looks irritated
at having to work on Friday
the 5th of July
I am working too
and from the bus window
I see the empty four-day weekend
streets of lower Manhattan
the pigeons feast undisturbed
in the sidewalk triangle
near the Chinatown Monument
although what they are pecking at
is invisible to me
slim pickings in the early
pre-tourist hours
the courthouse buildings

are deserted
the streets are so empty
we have not hit a stoplight
all the way downtown

83

Mini-Murphy Bus Service
Allen Malls sign
bump balump babump
smoke from BUG pipe
explosion in Coney Island
white stripe dividing lines
green tree and imitation old-time
lamppost
pukey feeling in gut
quiet tombstone of a bus
glass delivery truck
Beraios Transportation Service
small Asian woman
with bulging recycling shopping
cart
red light - we go through it
Sun Sing Theatre
Wing Shing Lei Toy Store
Yung Sun Restaurant
pigeons at the uptown bus stop
pigeons perched like
ornamental stonework
on Chinatown WW II monument
Citibank
Superhair
Rokkas' Coffee Shop
Another bus to Battery Park City
US Courthouse
government workers departing the bus
small crippled guy with

beret and headphones
substantial older woman in
sneakers, madras shirt
and babushka
tall man in gray
black man with cooler
Federal Building under construction
sporting strips of bright green
neon around its park benches
and orange plastic netting draped
over stacks of equipment
and supplies
morning bagel truck
at the corner
does brisk business

84

Another lucky morning
I slide onto the bus
like an Allen Street snake
the median park is littered
with bark and debris
left by yesterday's bad storm
everyone is sleeping
under and atop soggy cardboard
today will call for new box forays

no trees are down
only humans
and I am happy about those trees
because they survived
without the protection of forest company

muggy atmosphere
people moving slowly
as if pushing though thick sludge

a boy was swept away
last night in an angry
New Jersey riptide
this sort of thing
is becoming a common occurence
is Mother Nature hungry for
young blood?

he was revived
after cardiac arrest
and like my trees
on Allen Street he may live
to forget
the story

85

The day before I turn another
year older
David says "don't worry
you are young
don't worry
you look young
don't worry"
we both look young
I wasn't worried when
he said those things

this bus is very realistic
with sunlight of July dappling
across the seats
everybody dressed neat when we
should still be in pajamas
a black pigeon with red feet
pecks in the remains
of debris mixed with water
thrown out at the Chinese

vegetable stand

I have no watch today
but I am sure
we have made it to work
in record time
about 4 minutes from Houston
to the Federal Building

Life could be a little slower
and so could this
but

86

A gorgeous bright clear day
for the celebration of my
birth
although down south
an early hurricane has already
claimed 4 lives and is gathering
strength
while last night there was
a blood bath in Queens

the bus is crowded and I am
squeezed into the back row
of 5 seats which are not
big enough to hold the
average-sized American

for my birthday
I will go to work
I am a captive
of the work ethic
I will go out for lunch and dinner
with female friends and then

I will go home alone
at work I will be alone
but not quite so lonely

men never look at me anymore
only unsuspecting bus dispatchers
and drivers
for a minute or two

On the bus
I make my birthday wish
looking at men
dressed in ski parkas in July
dressed in baseball caps
pompous and puffed up
or sad and crumpled
in their seats
the sun is kind to us
and we are bathed in
gentle streaks
I will not say
what my wish is
I believe in old wives tales
including the one
that says if you tell your wish
out loud
it will never come
true

87

I am one year older
than I was two days ago
chronologically
but mentally
nothing has changed
I guess the bus 4550

was late this morning
because I see all the people
who usually ride earlier
maybe it's the beginning of one
of those days

Big Bertha the hurricane
is heading our way
reminding me of Bertha Bump
the store clerk of my childhood
we always made fun of
Big Bertha Bump

she wore her name tag
on her Woolworth's vest
back when it was called a
"five and dime"
now the five is worthless
and the dime is less than the five
used to be

Smashing Pumpkins keyboard player
OD'ed in his hotel room last
night
I say "congratulations!"
you made it
July 11
while everyone else
was worried about the weather
you may never have to
feel the rain again
unless of course
hell is only repetitious infinity
of impending hurricanes
which is more likely than not
I am still here
not worrying too much
more concerned about

work than
love or death
or beauty
or why the fans
rioted last night at
Madison Square Garden

88

Redrum is the word
on the street
somebody OD'ed
on Redrum
murdeR brand
I wonder why it is suddenly
so potent
somebody died
and all the junkies
in the Tri-state area
flock to the Lower East Side
looking for
Redrum
that little white powder
with the big kick in the
head
that will take you
over to the other side
with no return ticket

I used to get a brand called
Black Sunday
I liked it because
its name agreed with my
black sunday
soul
its effect forced any day

to release its grip
around my neck

the bus has already passed
the methadone clinic
I didn't check to see if the line
had dwindled
if all the imprisoned clients
had gone off in search
of immortality

89

I was at the bus stop for a long time
waiting
when a City Hall bus finally arrives
the dispatcher asks "what took so long?"
"I don't know" the driver answers
and we all get on
including the lady who still had
the Sale sign on the bottom of her shoe
who looks lost and who is doing
an unintentional imitation of
Minnie Pearl

I am hot
it's not too cool in this bus
and there are a lot of passengers
so I got stuck again
in the back row of five seats of which
the two on either end
don't have enough space
to fit my legs so--
I am in the middle seat
the one that is barely useable
these are the hot seats
under which I think

the engine for the A/C
is churning
it seems that must be it because
these seats are never
hot in the winter
when we could use it
my rear is warming up
and beads of sweat are
dripping into my eyes

but why am I complaining?
my back hurts and I should be happy
to be riding
on a moving heating pad
with built-in massage

90

Today is not a bad day
it is a really bad one
the weather is way beyond
miserable keeping us from
sweating with its water laden
particulate effrontery
it has been announced that
tomorrow will be even worse
cooler more humid
and thunderstorms
just in time for my carnival show
and it's also depressing as
the day after another plane
disaster TWA Boeing 747 from JFK
exploded over Long Isiand
coming down into the drink
in a million flaming shards
we are still searching for
survivors

If we find one
a human who lived
after dropping 13,000 feet
into the Atlantic Ocean
having just experienced
five explosions
in a fireball,
that person would be God
because from the moment
the news hit the airwaves
I knew that everyone was
dead
we are afraid of a terrorist
bombing
a land-to-air missile
we are waiting now for the call
taking credit
or the forensic proof
of evil intent

91

Oh gray misery
burn away this heavy
blotting of my sun
I think we have had enough rain
everything is coming up
moldy
poisonous mushrooms popping out
from lawns in places
where this type of mushroom
hasn't been
seen since first imported to
America in 1966

across the aisle
a woman paints her face

somehow in this
bumpling
no one has yet invented
a word good enough to describe
the scrambling your insides
take inside a shaky M-15 bus

I need a nice day for my show
nobody will come if it rains
it's supposed to be lucky
but my mind is too limited
to see what kind of
happy fortune
could result from a torrential
downpour
in NYC

92

First day back to work
after nine days
of freedom
feels like first day
of summer school
first day of college excitement
that will end
with a huge pile of papers
on my desk
and a thousand requests
for guidance and information
but I am happy
for the moment
now passing Canal Street

thinking about why my
fiction writing instructor
doesn't like me as the bus

rambles down East Broadway
at 7:16 AM
Good, I will be early
and can take time to prepare myself
for the day
the pigeons are happy too
picking at a breakfast
of invisible crumbs
probably leftover rice
donated by an anonymous
Chinese restaurant

we are in the final approach pattern
with all the recent bombings
TWA and Atlanta
one can only hope
the Federal Building gauntlet
that I must traverse
after I disembark
will not be targeted
for destruction this
morning

93

large rusted sewer pipes
have been exhumed
they are piled
in the Allen Street Median Park
waiting for reassignment
a gaping trench is fenced off
with un-biodegradable orange plastic
netting
this was where the pipes spent
the last 80-100 years
from the looks of them
I don't believe they have yet

been replaced
the sewage is pipe-less
the rain today will fill the hole
unearthing
underground mysteries
bodies of rats
or bones of humans

Olympic Park in Atlanta
will reopen today
a show of strength
lack of fear of terrorism
while in NYC
three suitcases left in
St. Patrick's Cathedral
were investigated by the
bomb squad
the police said last year
the same suspicious bags
would have simply been
stolen

94

On the last day of July
at 7:10 AM bus 4830
we have 74° and drizzle
humidity is at 90%
torrential downpours are possible
my spirit is not dampened
I have no appointments to keep
after work and am running
on Motrin to handle
wet weather's inevitable increase
in pain
the bus dispatcher is thin
and hides under the bodega awning
well it looks like a bodega

but I think it is run by Iranians
just as all the Italian Pizza Parlors
are now owned and run by Greeks
so the bodegas have become
Indian, Iranian, Arabian
and other Middle Eastern or
otherwise exotic tribes
The awning may be protecting
the dispatcher but with this
drizzle it is hard to say
it seemed to flow horizontally
into my face
but now I am safe inside 4830
safe, that is, unless the driver
has planted a suicide pipe bomb
inside the steering column

95

A low flying seagull makes
a garbage run up First Avenue
its shadowed wingspan giving
the illusion of covering
the street from sidewalk to sidewalk
until the whiteness of the bird
is consumed within our early morning
fog and pollution

More bodies have been recovered
from the ocean floor
a plane was forced to land in Philly
when smoke filled the cabin
many continuing passengers
waited for the bus to NYC

Olympic athletes
weep in defeat or jubilation

they have been heard to say
they feel dead relatives
are watching over them
most likely this sensation
is caused by the presence of Valkyries
waiting to carry dying soldiers
off to heaven

96

I had a long wait for PA 1662
twenty-five minutes during which five
South Ferry's passed before a single
City Hall which was of course
packed with seat hogs

These are the people that sit on the
outside of a two-person seat,

requiring newly arriving passengers
to crawl over them awkwardly
while the bus lurches away

while waiting, I saw all the
happy young couples descending
today into the ground
they looked so satisfied
I am not
my state of mind could
be compared to that of the
tall blond prostitute who upon
arriving at the far corner
of Allen Street
was whistled down by her pimp
or was it her john
an older black man in a baseball cap
with a white towel over his shoulders

she hustled her long emaciated frame
across to meet him on First Avenue
where she leaned on him to remove
a stone from her four-inch
stiletto shoes
and walked off with a great deal
of exaggerated hip movement

the part of this scene
with which I identify is the
stone in the shoe
certainly not the hip action
or the anorexia
the young couples did not have
stones in their footwear or if
they did were oblivious to it

There has been a creaking sound from below
along with groaning from the steering wheel
and related components

One seat hog exits now from
this creaking monster brute of a bus
her hogism no longer matters
because we are at Canal and rarely
pick up any more passengers
between here and the
end of the line

97

There is a small dead animal
in the road
most likely a cat
who tried in vain
for a tenth life

I watch the carcass and the traffic
for a few minutes, nothing happens
even huge trucks manage to avoid it
then it takes seven or eight
major hits in a row
reminding me of what I will become
today at work
a living being
flattened by supervisors
with diagnosable psychiatric illnesses
I will take hit after hit
it won't matter
that at some point
I become a limp cadaver
they will continue to
rip at my hide
until it is transformed into a shredded
pile of gray fur

Worth Street is up ahead
and I have a killer
stomachache

98

sky is a mishagosh
this morning
I know what that means
having had two Jewish ex-boyfriends
Greek and Puerto Rican boyfriends
and a Sicilian stalkee or two
has given me that extra flavor
in my linguistic skills
and it is,
the sky, a mess

I am waiting for another bomb
make it three
so we can have a peaceful
interlude from all this
terroristic egotism

Street crews are out early
from my bus window on M-15 2541
with the Buddha guy driver
shiny head
mountainous stomach
calm expression probably
brought on by
an extremely high dosage
of prescription valium
I see the workers pushing around
a few pebbles with a big broom

The man in the seat across from me
has been rethreading his tie
for ten minutes, for almost the whole ride
he finally gets it right,
rearranges his suspenders
while shaking his leg spasmodically
he asks his female companion
if she is result-oriented
then loosens his tie
and starts all over again

99

Although I am late today
I waited for another bus
got on the 8209 limited
passing up a standing room only
I don't feel good enough

to stand all the way
downtown

and besides
there is a very handsome
male riding in the seat
I had wanted for myself
something good to look at
which with my list
of requirements doesn't happen
much anymore
he has a pink bag
swinging between his legs
his breakfast no doubt--
I see the top of an orange juice
but the bag swinging
as it is and where it is
makes him all the more masculine
the imagery he unintentionally creates
of a giant set of pink balls
his hair is wet and slicked back
oh now, don't worry
the end of the ride is approaching soon
and there is not enough time
to fall in love...

100

There is an ozone alert
visible pollution touches down
and trails up First Avenue
cloaking the tall buildings in Midtown

when we reach Canal Street
I look out the bus window toward
Brooklyn
and see the sky above the bridge

is an evil yellow-gray
this is what we are breathing today
not air

At the bus stop there were
cigarette smokers who will not be
bothered with the diluting effect of
oxygen today
In the seat in front of me a young
business woman, who had switched buses
in Chinatown, unless she was most
unlikely looking Methadone Clinic customer I
have ever seen,
pops a Cert
I watched her toss away a Virginia Slim
as she boarded
The smell wafting from her was not
Cert correctable, it clung to her hair
her clothes and generally poisoned
the air around her body

Little Vance
has been roused by his mother
so we are all awake now
some of us look more eager than others
to depart this air conditioned-halfway-
decent-atmosphere-for-breathing bus
and begin our trudge through
the covert deadly ozone cloud hazard
to get somewhere we don't really
want to be anyhow--work

101

Two men get out of a cab
they are telling the driver how great he is

the Asian cabby pulls away smiling
shaking his head
one of the men, maybe from the Islands
or Africa, says something to the other
who is dressed in the
usual teenage hip hop uniform
and raises a threatening hand bringing
it down with great force,
stopping a quarter inch from the
hip hop guy's head
who apparently gave the cab driver
too much money

The bus stop is busy today
the dispatcher (of whom I have not
seen hide nor hair for at least a week)
spots the little shrunken man
who used to walk the grizzled black dog
until it died, who might well be
an ex or current junkie, given the
caved in appearance of his jaw
caused by missing teeth, the dispatcher
observes him setting a small
brown paper bag (coffee and a roll?
OJ and a doughnut?) down on a ledge
before disappearing
into the Iranian Bodega to buy his
morning paper
The dispatcher goes over and snatches
the bag, hiding it behind his bulky
blue uniformed body
I'm watching the whole incident
and he puts on the greatest deadpan
face ever
the guy with the shrunken head
stumbles out of the bodega
in flapping brown shoes
and yells at the dispatcher

to give it up
by now the dispatcher has placed
the bag on the public telephone stand
and positioned himself in front of it
Mr. Shrunken Head reaches around
him and grabs the bag
"I saw you out of the corner of my eye,"
he says. He points to his eyebrow,
flashes a toothless smile,
and gives an impish wink--
he has made the dispatcher's day
and I think this sullen stone-faced city
employee might be
a lot nicer than he look

102

I am moving at breakneck speed
after waking up an hour and fifteen minutes
after the alarm
I can still arrive at work on time
with any luck
the bus is cool
but is outfitted
with Plexiglas windows
that have been marred repeatedly
by low hanging tree branches
and other
scrapes with the universe
they are so cloudy
I can't make out the passing scenery

Lots of Asians
are riding downtown today
I wonder if any of them will get off
at Chinatown or will they continue
on to work in City Hall,

the courthouses
or Federal Plaza

Usually no one gets off in Chinatown
except to visit the Methadone Clinic
where there is no line today
It's probably too late and the clients
are all on the job, back home or gone to school

Two Asians actually depart the bus
at the far
edge of Chinatown
for exotic jobs I hope
the rest of us continue down the tubes
into the bowels of lower Manhattan
to toil for the government or
to feed or clothe those who do

103

It's raining,
so this must be the day
I have to go outside and keep
appointments
that was my first thought
after my feet hit the floor

The bus driver kindly waits for me
when he sees me running
wipers are squeaking over the
front end panorama
It is dark from hanging clouds
foreshadowing winter
a medium heavy downpour
is underway
It is 62° so I have worn
my leather parka

which is too warm but
should keep me partly dry
my pants are soaked through
from the knee down
I'm sure glad I wore my boots
but I wish it was a little colder

104

Horrible traffic problems have
been reported the last two mornings
A garbage truck overturned and
blocked off the Verrazano Narrows Bridge
on Tuesday
Today a huge slab of concrete
fell off a flatbed truck
on the Cross Bronx Expressway
making me feel justified
for all those times
I warned someone
who was driving me somewhere
not to tailgate a truck of manure
a car transport or a hillbilly vehicle
piled with rickety furniture
while going seventy mph
following the old theory
that any object balancing at the
edge of another object somewhere
above the ground while going
at high speeds
will fall on you

does a crate of chickens
smash through a windshield if
nobody lives to squawk about it?
another traffic mishap tomorrow
will make it three days in a row

that should be the end of it
No such problems on M-15 No. 4544
a flawless ride was enjoyed
by all

105

A bum in City Hall Park
told me "You look nice in that suit"
this is the first pleasant comment
I have had from the street in many years
it made my yesterday
but today is here again and
I am spending time contemplating
the state of the inside of a
Manhattans pigeon's stomach
after watching one peck at
smashed things and bits of glass
it found on the bus stop sidewalk

Last night, while I was waiting for
the M-9 under the view of
a golden-winged statue
that inflamed the downtown sky
with dazzling reflections of the setting sun
a sparrow landed near me
It landed several times...
at least I think it was the same sparrow
it flew in wide circles from traffic
sign to median tree
only to put down in the street
in front of me again
and cock its head at me
it was a very thin sparrow
I wondered if it was waiting for me
to dole out some crumbs

Self-portrait Polaroids, converted to grayscale

some food, or if he was the
spirit of my guardian angel
foreshadowed by the towering
gilded statue before the darkening sky
sent to give me a message
to let me know
that he would always be there
otherwise, why would he spend his time
in the middle of east Broadway
when there was a beautiful lawn
of young green grass
only inches away?

Then I remembered how the rats
run through the park at night
and realized
the lawn must be full of poison
or only fake sod with no worms
or contaminated worms

Aw who cares anyway?
after all a sparrow is really
just a flying rat anyway

106

A big fight is in progress
between store owners at the bus stop
about who is responsible
for a rotting smelly mound of garbage
I happen upon this scene, angry already
because the garbage truck
is now blocking most of the bus stop
while the garbage obstructs the rest
so I can't run for my bus
and miss it by two seconds

I arrive in time to see the
sanitation engineers refusing to
pick up the disgusting load of crap
which all reminds me of
Pineapple boy - Bob Dole
whose very name nauseates me
who accepted the Republican nomination
last night
like we didn't know he would
I seriously hope his is a lost cause
this bid for the presidency
by a man who would institute
the Amerikan caste system
might as well just pull the chain, Pineapple boy
if we wind up with you
we know where the USA is going

107

I was almost run down by a car today
I'm looking left because a bike rider
is coming the wrong way
I estimate he will arrive at the spot
in the crosswalk
where I am planning to step
at exactly the same instant
I attempt to depart
the sidewalk
So I make my move cleverly
stepping off the curb with the intention
of speeding up my pace
Then from the right, slicing over four lanes
of Houston Street traffic
a car passes two inches from my toes
he honked,
but only at the last possible second

timing it perfectly
to scare me out of my wits
I yelled the usual expletives
and proceeded to Allen Street
where though alive by only the
skin of my teeth
like the golfer who drives his shot
into a hole behind a stand of trees
and fights all and sundry type of adversity
to get on the green with a chance of making
par
then doesn't even come close to sinking the
putt,
the powers that be
still made me run in front
of a wall of oncoming speeding vehicles
to try against all odds
to make my bus

108

The wind is high
I miss one bus and wait twenty-five minutes
for the next
I watch the smokers sucking in
one last breath of exhaust
before descending into the subway
as if the air down there
was so clean and fresh
they would immediately expire
while detoxing
without a good supply of smoke
in their lungs

The dispatcher has his car parked

at the stop
There is a miniature crown
in the back window
and a sign that reads
Official Business
The dispatcher is on the pay phone
when I arrive and when I leave
he has let the phone hang down from
its metal cord while he says something
to our driver
she responds "I don't care, that's
why they pay you the big bucks
to come and see what I want"

My shoulder blade hurts deep inside
it is cold out but also hot and muggy
80's are predicted, 90's for tomorrow
The first unbearably hot day of summer
with two weeks to go until Labor Day
My radio announcer says with disgust
"Summer has finally decided to make
an appearance" I guess he doesn't
remember last summer when all
those people died in the Chicago heat wave
I prayed for this cool summer
wanted to make it through another one

Margo Hemingway is ruled
a barbiturate overdose
now the only question is
did she do it herself or did
someone help her out
Miss Universe has been directed
to lose weight (27 pounds)
or relinquish her crown
She currently weighs 130
she is so overweight,
so tremendously flabby and bulbous

that I have to think
what is this world coming to?

109

Our first dog day has arrived
all the dogs will want to stay inside
the day smells like a dead mackerel
if only it were a fish so I could
throw it back
muggy thickness coats lower Manhattan
people trying to mask the odor
have on too much perfume
too much aftershave
which overwhelms
the feeble attempt of oxygen
to put in a brief
early morning appearance

Of course, on the bus,
PA 1601 with its decrepit gum wad
blotted floor
the guy across from me sneezes 8 times
in rapid succession from a horrible
summer cold
there is no place for me to move
luckily he gets off
managing to bash me in the leg
with his gym bag so I will
have his cold germs and a throbbing knee
to remind me of how the MTA
air conditioning wasn't working
right today and how I am
sitting in a swamp up to my eyeballs
and how all these people are really
alligators and are prepared

to snap off my nose
the dogs are yapping and jumping
up to eat this day
good for them I say
no one else would be able
to swallow it

110

The Stella D'Oro delivery guy
wears a button on his safety belt
that reads: Hoffa in '96"
The color of the summer trees
has faded
they are covered with soot
and other toxic city chemicals
and have weathered ozone alerts
and temperature inversions
TWA tests have not proved sabotage
though witnesses insist a missile
brought the plane down
Upon first hearing their accounts
as given to ghoulish TV anchor persons
I thought of a missile
but wondered who would have the
connections to obtain such
high-powered weaponry
to launch off the coast of Staten Island
or from a small boat in the ocean.
Some foreign government?
certainly not some schleppy ex-husband
of a stewardess in search of large
insurance proceeds

A fire rages uptown - a 5 alarmer
I was roused from sleep at 1:41 AM

by sirens and a heavy smoke condition
in my nighttime bedroom air
It may have been burning until now
or perhaps the Lower East Side has countered
with a local conflagration
At the bus stop it was more obvious
than usual that we are engulfed in a city
of structural defects further suffering the
insidious action of unobstructed urban decay

111

Coming off a lost weekend of
Flexeril and Motrin taken Friday night,
on Monday morning I am still out of it
and I feel my back pain returning
In the future I will choose pain
when the alternative is so empty

We have bright sunshine
but muggy conditions
I am late and must take advantage of
any small bursts of energy
like this morning's brief flash
to clean the bird cages after
stepping in sunflower husks
for two days
and not caring really about
the diabetic complications
of a foot puncture wound.

My cyber boyfriend
has turned out to be a drip
he is tattooed,
but only by female artists
he has piercings,

but doesn't wear the jewelry much
he got pissed off when I sent an e-mail
telling him he can not sleep at my house
how could I think that he would
even imply such a thing?
he may never contact me again
he went off in a cyber huff
I guess he doesn't know anyone
like all of my old boyfriends

112

The bus smells of cheap perfume
the side panel is boiling hot
on my arm
it is 7:05 AM on the 1589
southbound to City Hall
people chatter away in the back
but it is beyond my powers to speak
I could only croak at the nice man
who held the door of my apartment
building open this morning
somehow, we have reached the stoplight
at East Broadway in one minute

Today I saw a large sticky mousetrap
with two dead mice and twenty or so
dead cockroaches
which brings to mind Saturday's
conversation in the trendy new
health food store on Avenue A
One woman was against the snap trap
but the others all said give me the
snap trap
before the sticky trap any day
as they spoke they continually

smoothed their tattooed bare arms
and rotated their facial piercings
while ignoring the customers
at the register
if I were a mouse, I would not
want my fate to rest in their hands
they can't even make change
for a bean sprout sandwich

113

I am very late but catch the 8209
within moments of arrival at the bus stop
It's 7:40 AM
I have experienced a dead mouse delay
found it under a chair near
my front door
I finally understood the disgusting
odor in my apartment over the
last few days
now it is the bus that smells heavily
of garlic

While I waited for the bus, I watched
a huge bird circling above First Avenue
disappearing in and rematerializing out
of a low hanging mixture
of smog and clouds
The bird was very large and reminded
me of the Eastern Condor,
or as less glamorous named,
the Turkey Vulture
that is attracted by the flesh of roadkill
in the country
I know a recently deceased body
has attracted this raptor to

First Avenue

The bus ride is a long one
I am in the back far right corner
where I have to put my feet up
on the hump formed by the inside
wheel guard in order to perch
uncomfortably
no one gets off, so I am stuck there
like the used paper towel
that is stuck in the vent
next to me above the emergency exit
release sign blowing whatever germs
it carries all over me
invisibly
the garlic stench has become intolerable
the guy who ties his tie
for the whole trip is riding across
from me - tying his tie
straightening his pants
fixing his collar
my stop appears on the horizon
hallelujah I say
I will make it off of here
without puking.

114

my head is on wrong
is not balanced properly atop
my shoulders
it is full of pressure
not helped at all by
the presence of
a smoke-drenched man
who smells like

he has already sucked in twenty
cigarettes by 6:58 AM
he slams himself down next to me
allowing his musty fumes to encase me
I am happy to learn that I still have
my sense of smell
though a more gentle
awakening to this fact
would have been appreciated
lilac toilet water or the delicate scent of
a single yellow rose
would have been preferred
the president is promising
to crack down on cigarettes
but everything has its negative consequences
what will all the cancer doctors do
if early agonizing deaths no longer
support their homes and swimming pools
and the hospitals are no longer
overcrowded with wheezing lungers
the social security rolls will swell
to the bursting with all the healthy retirees
the recovering drug addicts might drown
in coffee

I am relieved from this line of useless
speculation by flashes of color
out the bus window
where ancient members
of the Asian downtown exercise
group manipulate red paper fans
in circular motion
In spite of the stale air in which
I am presently held captive
I can see that the outside air
is as fresh as a daisy

I wait in a fishbowl today
watched by a wild-looking character
parked at the bus stop in a decaying
red vinyl chair
he also conducts
drug transactions
pees behind the dumpster
and begs for cigarettes

outside the Iranian bodega
he watches as four buses pass
not going my way
he and the drivers withering me
with superior smirks

I am relieved now
out of the reach of close scrutiny
safely seated on #4316
among my fellow passengers
here in this miniature democracy
of egomaniacs, self-centered
miserable paranoids like me,
who don't even look up

The distorted self spit up to counteract
this early morning
watching of the specimen
is slipping back inside
the jarred edges of the day
mesh and start to clear
A storefront sparkles and I am rescued
by a vision

Once again it is the day after
Labor day and I have lost another summer
I feel as if I must go to Woolworth's
and buy a notebook for the
fall semester even though I have
not been to school in 25 years.

The boss has returned from his vacation
my stomach cringes
he will reduce me to tears before the end of
this day
I must remember it is Tuesday and
I can stand anything for 4 days

It is almost fall and we are in the hottest
days of summer, newscasters marvel at the
weather but I know it is no different
from many recent years where Winter
has juxtaposed with Summer leaving
no Fall in-between

Fall is my season
that is why they have canceled it again
it suits my hair and my skin
ideal for wearing leather and taking
marathon walks across the city
but I am prisoner on PA 1704
the bus to 4 days in Hell
it will plunge me into infernal regions
where a madman reigns and I am a
high-ranking crispy critter
nothing is quite good enough for him
real life is obliterated
I disintegrate inside his apoplectic screaming

Yes this is the bus to Hades
cleverly concealed to resemble any other
mild-mannered M-15 to City Hall

117

Black day lined with black Hefty bags
rubble strewn trenches
Chinese delivery trucks
independent garbage trucks
school buses yellowing every corner
7:00 AM - too early for unloading
one forklift skitters out of Ho King warehouse

what isn't black is gray
bleak dampness is not lifting
a pigeon narrowly escapes death
by rear-view mirror

red light
white pigeon flying
white seagull flying
loud mouth passenger's angry voice
explodes
waking us
she and her companion
have already been at the bottle
light rain spots the front windshield
no umbrellas are yet in sight

The rain has begun already though
not predicted
this day will not be pussy-footing around
the bus stinks of garlic and aftershave

I jumped up from bed last night
to write a letter to the ghost
of Herbert Huncke
and accidentally pulled my arm
out of its socket
lack of sleep has me seeing trails
of day-glo green
around a white pigeon

Park trees brandish ugly leaves
like rust
not autumn color
black, brown and yellow deadness
shriveling
too soon

This day sucks, making it
two in a row
it is punishment enough to be
forced to work on 2 hours sleep
why am I also forced to breathe air
that is acting like mud
to be stuck inside this clammy skin
over which no type of garment
can be comfortable
why am I sitting here smelling
someone's god awful BO
wondering if I did the right thing
by giving that cyber guy with ten tattoos
my telephone number
and why do I feel guilty for not

bringing many tins of fancy feast
to the driveway to save my
neighborhood's host
of skinny stray cats?

119

Graffiti truck crosses Grand Street
like a giant canvas
in the very modern museum
surrounded by random decay
in the cool air which feels hot
on account of extreme saturation

Hi-lo's rule the dawn
cutting off our driver's attempt
to take his shortcut at the
Mobil Station
near the sign of the flying horse
the Mobil Pegasus
that Basquiat and Warhol
painted in and then painted
back out
the artists have quickly joined the
demolished symbol
the canvas outliving all three
of them
gasoline itself may be the next casualty

Our arrival at Worth Street
is looming
the job approaches
hidden behind the massive
Federal Building complex
but I know it's there
waiting to swallow me and cripple me
in my office with its fancy

but unserviceable leather chair

Street cleaning crews cheerfully
discuss assignments while expertly handling
their brooms and long-handled dust-pans
by afternoon, Hurricane Fran will be
messing up the situation and they
might not look so happy

120

Seagulls perch on
the tall streetlamps
dotting the median divider
on Houston Street
one is bobbing his head
so intensely I am captured
in the action and
narrowly miss stepping
in some foul garbage
on the sidewalk

I am in a good mood
feeling thin
thinking of my approaching date
with a man with ten tattoos
and one body piercing
I have seventeen and one body
piercing
we might be twins
but he is ten years younger
which possibly means
I need three more tattoos
he claims my age is a positive thing
maybe he thinks I will be easier to hold
tired of younger women

who don't share his views
on skin adornment

One seagull has taken flight
I see her in my mind
and imagine she is an albatross
come to give me good luck
and happiness
for all my future days

I think about this as the bus
cruises through Chinatown
feeling grateful I didn't kill the albatross
or kill myself and miss
this sliver of joy

121

I am in a great mood
happy to see Maggio Beef Trucks
spewing poisonous black smoke
into the spot where I will step off
the sidewalk
happy to see swarms of circling pigeons
and to worry about the bombs
they could drop on my good suit
happy to observe a long truck
covered in cow face paintings
do a wheelie from Houston onto Allen
tossing its huge back trailer tires
in my directions
causing me to retreat graciously from the
street at the bus stop
because I am in a good mood
I am not even upset about the guy
in front of me who has not bothered

to pick copious amounts of lint
off the back of his sweatshirt
I am not unhappy that my nose keeps
itching and will not desist
and it is all for a man
not even a real man
the thought of a man
and of talking to one
with stated intentions
what does he look like?
will keep me occupied today
even my boss will not be able
to ruin me
even if this bus turns at the
corner into infinity and never returns
I will not be shaken!

122

Never count on anything
the only constant is change
the only guarantee is death
the bus comes fast this morning
I cried my little heart out yesterday
over the unfortunate facts of my life
one of which is a rotten boss
who ruins my bus trip with the
thought that it is delivering me
into his orbit where
he will deal with me
on a subhuman level
and will become the next victim
in my book
while I work all the magick
in my power
to keep from jumping

over his desk
to snap his neck like a twig
or pound on his head with
his marble elephant figurine
I would feel sad if the elephant broke
but would revere it for its sacrifice
and
here I am once more being swallowed
by the downtown abyss
a saint about to be burned
in combat with the flamethrowing
beast
a saint who will fight by not fighting
and who will win by
concentrating on inner grace

123

The token box in our bus
is not working 4317
I've never seen anything like it before
confused, I wanted my money
14 dimes and 2 nickels
to go in and be counted,
but I merely added them to the pile
of quarters sitting on top of the
token slot
naked quarters
unsecured quarters
evidence of the end result
of mechanical failure
the news last night had stories
of the Chinatown sidewalk fish markets
how they collected the
bloody melted ice in buckets
and spilled it in the streets

allowing customers to pick through
the fillets with unwashed fingers
now the stands are empty
the wooden dividers packed with
pristine ice waiting to keep
the corpses cold
in the news film, one fish
was still alive
swimming at the top of
a white container
he flapped his tail
trying to turn and swim
like always to the bottom of
the river, lake, sea, ocean
but he will never even see
the bottom of the plastic bucket
that confines him
he is next on line for the
ice treatment
he will not care that the neighbors
have filed a petition
he will die today and his blood will be
emptied with the rest
onto East Broadway
his watered down blood
will spill into the gutter
and the news will not report it

124

This day is already living up
to dire predictions
the first bus had to be taken
out of service
I had a long wait with a heavy
travel bag which I could not put down

due to wet sidewalk conditions
I see the next bus is packed to
the gills and wait a few seconds
for yet the next one
which is deceptively empty
only when I get on do I discover that
the one passenger is really a two-headed
hydra - a loud mouth
screaming baby and its louder mouth
screeching mother
and who does it turn out to be
but Lance the baby who is usually
sound asleep
I must now admit that I like him much
better that way at this hour
he is drawing repeated blows from
his angry mother
and begins to throw a fit in his bus seat

I passed a pair of empty sneakers
black with a white boomerang design
they were sitting in the rain
next to a sodden pile of cardboard
outside the little park near Norfolk Street
they were exactly like mine.

125

The sun is out for the first time
in four days
I got to soak in a lot of those rays
to combat a buildup of dark depression
the young female bus driver
cheerfully announces the stops
to all six riders
If we pick anyone up it will be

at the Catherine Street
transfer point
I was up late talking to my
internet date
who says he loves women
with tattoos
he is so liberal about who he sees
it worries me
No additional passengers
board at Catherine
but we lose one and bring
our number down to five
hardly worth the trip
for the MTA
Here I am approaching the stop
for work again
gladder than usual

126

The man at the bus stop is talking
to two ladies
telling them how handsome he is
what a good lover he is
how he wants a rich woman
so they can watch TV together
and he will tickle her
he is 28 he says
and has given his seventh wife
nine babies

The two women,
one with short white hair
and a costume necklace,
the other in permed blond
and tan raincoat
look like they are listening avidly

Finally, one of them speaks:
"Why don't you go away now?
We've heard enough and we just
want a little slice of peace and quiet
in the morning"
He continues with his monologue

A teen girl with huge breasts
squeezed into a lowcut blouse
approaches
walking to school with a heavyset
girlfriend
the bus dispatcher who has been
looking uptown waiting for
the late bus turns as she passes
to check out the back of her
sausage skin bell bottoms
I shake my head
I know which one of the girls
he is watching
I think to myself that she is too young
to deal with such heated attention
but it's none of my business

I get on the bus
the drunk who has been haranguing
the two sainted ladies orders
the driver to take them
wherever they want to go.

127

Bus #1683, drive me all the way
to Key West, since we are already
headed in that direction
Take me away from my own head

I promise to throw it out the door
at the next stop as nourishment
for the rats and
pigeons if you agree to haul ass
and never come back
I will be ecstatic with no head
glad to ditch my brain
which is like a mosquito swamp
infecting me with malarial sweats
transporting me back repeatedly
to relive past disappointments
I will be grateful to have no eyes
let them flirt with the vermin
of the street and leave me the hell alone
stop them from showing me
faulty visions of other people
who appear to be continually having fun
while I have none
I will be pleased even to abandon my ears
and mouth
to escape from hearing more bad news
or scathing insults
I won't be able to stick my foot in
my mouth every time I want
to be eloquent

Hey driver!! Wait!! This is not the way
to Florida!
We are on Worth Street in NYC!!
I think you made a wrong turn at Canal!!

Cold mornings made colder for me
by better control of blood sugar concentrations
my teeth chatter when everyone else

looks comfortable in their light fall jackets

My most recent blind date
was so blind he did not show for our
appointment and did not call
Monday, Tuesday or Wednesday
as he said he might
Today he flies to Los Vegas
Sunday, I leave for Provincetown

Yesterday, the Yankees won their division title
for the first time in 15 years
I hope the Mick was watching them
get 19 runs in the first game and 6
in the second
My blind date was probably
at the game and later celebrating
while I forgot that they were playing
writing out applications for NYFA
Grants for David and I in non-fiction and
poetry

I finally slept good last night
after going to bed sick at heart
praying for a midnight phone call
that mercifully didn't come

129

Today I experienced life
as a sanitation engineer does
at the back end of the garbage truck
as I walked up to the bus stop
and was forced to pass through a cloud
of some vile dust that exploded
from a black shiny Hefty bag as it
was crushed in the gears

of the garbage grinder
I couldn't help but breathe in this
detria along with the rubbish disposal guys
dressed up in their green and orange outfits
for the occasion
I hope that dust wasn't asbestos or
kitty litter
as my lungs are already in poor
enough condition without added
chemical or waste product insult

The bus ride however, is very smooth
unlike last night's trip home
where I was sandwiched
between a family of five with a mini TV
who were watching Ricky Lake
I guess that show must be a
hard one to miss

130

Early rain
headlights reflect off a
shining Delancey Street
I am delayed
watching smoke curl up
from under the pavement
to outline and then enfold
a tree, leafless and skeletal
after this week's hurricane

Fork lifts move backward
like reversing break dancers
passengers discuss agencies
and holidays
East Broadway has been achieved

Radio City is burning
the Yankees won on account of
fan misadventure
and my blind date
still hasn't called.

131

The 1691 bus driver throws a fit
saying I put in $1.40 instead of $1.50
I know I counted this money twice
so he is fucked
someone before me or after me
put in less
or one dime did not register
but in our great city
there is no room for argument
If you wish to ride, you will pay
however, today, that is only after
asking the driver three times
to repeat what he has said
about my alleged shortfall
since he is deliberately
mumbling this information
beneath his breath
I am tired of all the shit
having had three bad days in a row
I can't take mini crap like this
to start a fourth sub standard day
from now on I will always use a token
they can't argue about that
and then I will be able to look out upon
my lovely October city scenes
in the only kind of infinitesimal peace
my rebellious mental contortions
will allow

instead of steaming furiously in
my seat writing surly bus driver
condemnations
and beaurocratic exposes
at 7:36 AM on Friday morning

132

The handsome guy
who looks like Bruce Willis
is sitting in the front of the bus
he is so cute
he usually talks to the driver
but today he is keeping his mouth shut

pollution is spewing
city school buses flood the streets
along with white Sanitation Department
grinders
It has been three days since I have
traveled this route
I guess although I hate it passionately
I also miss it

It is s frigid morning
my blood sugar is under 100 and dropping
the Yankees won the American League
pennant
a yellow newspaper delivery truck
is in action
the cute guy is still silent
the Say Eng Look restaurant
is enclosed behind
wooden construction barriers
the oriental exercisers in the park
all have one leg extended into the air

a Sabrett hot dog truck is making deliveries
and for this instant
and this instant only
all is right in
New York City

133

The revenge of
City Hall is
here – the South
Ferry passengers
are still waiting
I missed one bus
but got another
in less than three
minutes, Bruce
Willis is in the
front seat, so I
know I'm not too late –
Today he's deep
in conversation
with the driver
I wonder if he
is a driver too,
or just ultra
friendly, but
only to bus drivers
the clouds
are puffy sheep
floating innocently
above the
Manhattan iniquities
pigeons circle
Division St.
Also well above

the reach of our
despair
until they land
to be crushed
by the buses like this
one,
flattened into gray
lumps with
black and white stripes
sticking up from
their wings
but even so
their suffering
is limited
while ours is
infinite

134

Dark fog hangs in
viewed through scratched windows
of bus #2244
thousands of lines mar the Plexiglas and
suggest the wanton mutilation of tree branches
by large automotive devices
and their feeble but defacing
retaliation
East Broadway is a ghost town
only one or two walkers
solitary early morning
lights at the vegetable stand
provide the only bleak illumination

Pineapple boy did not win the debate
the President didn't lose it
nothing new has been said

the speechwriters have boring brains
the bridge to the 21st century
is already wearing thin
I spend hours on line
typing responses to strangers
in the Artists Cafe chat room
drinking imaginary cocktails
made of slashes and brackets
and shocking everyone with my
advanced age of forty-nine

135

Fall is throwing down its leaves
after tropical storm Josephine is completed
we will have a weekend fling with Lila
who will clean us and bare us for the next
round with Winter
who is hardly an old man, I think

The big red sun in the East appears to us
as a giant blinding disc bleeding into
the surrounding sky
through New York City's polluted
atmosphere
exhibiting a degree of beauty
seldom seen without the aid of
hazardous waste

Yesterday was a hot one but today
is cool again
the World Series begins tomorrow
afternoon
and I am wearing
leather

Day after bad rain
city is almost spotless
the traffic cops are still dressed
in orange plastic
we stand in humiliated defeat
as the NY Yankees were buried
says the Times headline
smashed into submission is my phrase
on the matter
hoards of people run around
the slick sidewalk maze
in a million different directions
the inside of my head feels
just like that
a metropolis of useless neuron impulses

The driver is a bit of a cowboy
and the supervisor on this bus #8486
is somewhat lacking
not to mention
the narrow bumpy streets of Chinatown

Black clouds cover the sky
seagulls turn in the air above
the criminal court building
downtown is here
my dreaming of lizards singing
Clara Clara is over

Windows shaped like fanned peacock tail
feathers
smoke on the horizon, floating in midair

love down the drain to nowhere nowhere
sucked away in a flash bolt, reality vanishes
normalcy was never really a possibility
bars on all the windows now
people want to steal everything
but crime is down since the deportation policy
on captured drug dealers
went into effect

Vicious slash red-deep
my heart is dried out
coagulated brown blood turns to dust
green construction barriers adorned with
yards of blue plastic ugly
eveything is so ugly
the passengers smell bad
I wonder why I bothered getting up
this morning

138

Token machine #9226 is broken
the dispatcher can't fix it, causing a delay
we'll be moving soon though
his name is Jack
after two years of standing at his stop
every day watching him chart the buses
and stare at pretty women
I finally know his name
because the driver said
"Thank you, Jack"
which goes to show that everything
will be revealed in time
Metrocard customers search for change
to drop in the machine
not even real cash money will go down

the slot
I'll laugh if the Command Center
breaks in today touting its virtues

The trees on Allen are almost bare
the driver out maneuvers truckers
who jockey their generic white delivery
vehicles with no regard for the other
traffic
trying to get as close to their destination
as possible
this bus is a jiggler - looks
modern enough but tosses us around like
an old nag on a hayride
skies are gray
a seagull views the downtown panorama
from a Chinatown streetlamp

139

Delancey & Allen
Next. Announces
the driver of 8203
as I slide carefully
in my seat
trying not to incite
the tendinitis
in my elbow
This could be a
good day
the World Series
is a gut wrencher
the weather is
cool
My arm hurts less
nobody can decide

what to wear
a would-be drummer
taps out a
furious beat with his fingers
somewhere in the
back of the bus
we're passing Canal St.
I dream of spending
my evening
talking to
other pierced and
tattooed people on
the internet, the
same people who
never talk to
me in person
if they can help it
they're fun
sometimes talk dirty
give me a much
appreciated thrill
that I don't
often experience
in the flesh
I am attracted to few
One ex-junkie with
AIDS, who is a tall Stallone
One door installation
mechanic tall with
a pony tail
One old and weird looking
Hispanic bus dispatcher
named Jack
my choices are limited
but the bus will
still take me where
I have to go

140

The boys of summer
are all my rage
as my simple heart
is brightened
over the outcome
of a national sporting
event where
men chase a ball
around a grass
and dirt diamond
before millions of spectators
Last night the
Bronx Bombers
won the fifth game
of the 1996 World Series
in Atlanta, their
third win in a row
and come home
to NYC to try
and capture the
pennant for the
first time since
1978. Back when I was
a kid, nobody
else ever won
the W.S.
but I am not a
kid and everything has changed

141

Crappy day
bus #9195
day before downtown

World Series parade
2 days after
6 hour test
for work that
disintegrated
my weekend
one day after
unexpected visit
to Native American
Museum
where I bought
a book
The Creeks and the Seminoles
to try and sort out
my ancestors
the only ones I
can get a real
handle on
The Irish ones are
too obscure
apparently coming here
to work on the
Erie Canal
after the Irish
potato famine.
But the Indian ones
and I say Indian
because there is
now a movement in
the NA community
to reclaim the name
Indian
have names going
back to the French
and Indian wars
and I know the
clan was
the Wind Clan

and I know of
ancestor in the everglades
but I am afraid
to question my mother
who does not encourage
this interest of mine
in her father's heritage
The downtown
triangles of office buildings
loom ahead
history will have to wait.

142

It's not 7 AM yet
very early today –
combination of
the recent change to
Daylight Savings
The Yankee parade
in the canyon of heroes
and news of broken
water mains in Canal St.
has inspired me
to get moving
at this ungodly hour
After receiving not one
IM on the internet
all weekend, last
night I was talking
to 3 guys at once
as well as the chat room
which proves I can
be popular
when I'm invisible
driver nearly

flips the bus
turning on East Broadway
last night a
plane landed
on its belly at JFK
3 passengers injured
sliding down the
emergency chute
I hope this cowboy
driver gets us
downtown without
forcing us to climb
out the windows
Lunch will be a bust
today the streets
will be packed with
jubilation
and I will have
to go hungry

143

The clean up
operation went
on through the
night
We will see how
good they did
at sweeping up
miles of shredded
paper and other evidence
of human inhabitation
McDonalds wrappers
soda and coffee
cups, cigarette butts
and the like

Whatever was
missed will surely
wind up in
the river,
carried there by
today's furious wind
that was tossing
rubbish in
the air on Houston St.
I wonder if the
baby lived
born an orphan
after its
mother was killed
by a car
on the news
Clinton and Pineapple
Boys are portrayed
as criminals
and the government
claims an 8 month
old fetus was killed
by an airbag

144

Halloween
Scream
start my day with
a lidocaine
injection in my elbow
a brace for my arm
and a new anti-inflammatory
feels better already
Writing is painless
as I watch hordes
of school children

dressed in plastic
pumpkin suits
on their little
spook parades
later on I will be
assailed by
ballerinas, devils,
draculas and ghosts
who walk the
streets looking
for a dime for candy
already a trick
even with the treat
I will run home
from work on
the uptown M-9
so there is less
chance of a random
massacre that
could occur when the
kiddies push me
to the breaking
point
and I would not
want a black eye
or broken eggshell
up my nose
like I got one year
innocently crossing
2nd Avenue wearing
my vampire teeth
traffic is impossible
due to construction
work in progress at
Grand St. – usually
this is dormant
when I go by at 7 AM
but it is 10:05

the sun is bright
the leaves
are sparse now on
the trees
as we prepare to
navigate the
sea of delivery trucks
in Chinatown
bananas hang in
neat arrangements
in the fruit stand
all the markets are
open, and residents
are filling up dozens
of pink bags
that they will later
pile at their feet
in the bus
blocking the aisles
for the unhealthier
passengers
the trucks cause
some delay, but not
as much as the old man
with a walker
departing the bus
at Catherine St.
We head toward
the snarl of
vehicles in the
courthouse area
Federal Plaza
brings in thousands
every day – an
ambulance and 10
police cars loom on
the Worth St. horizon
honking music is

in the air
mixing with the
too loud headphone
walkman beat behind
me
hopefully we'll get
through this
quickly – I can see
my stop across
the way –
who knows when I
will finally arrive
there?

145

My spirit guide
is a wolf and though
he let me pet
him Sunday morning
and trailed along
behind me all day
he is no
longer tangible
I have felt
him snarling both
within me and
without me since I was young
but I have never seen
him before now
I am of
the Wind Clan
but an unknown
male ancestor
has recently been
added to the mix,
maybe he was

Wolf I don't know
the wind is
still today
the wolf is longing
to be held tight
like a pet do

146

Election Day
the farce is in full swing
I am so glad that by tomorrow we will not
have to hear Pineapple Boy's nasty voice again
He will lose, for all the wrong reasons of
course
he will lose because he is old
because he has a crippled hand
because the sound of him grates unmercifully
nobody wants a president like that
In this nation we would vote for the Devil
before picking a chump who would not
present a pretty picture
to the rest of the world

It's late
I had to vote by paper ballot
and it took more time than pulling a lever
but I feel better because I know I have
signed something in my own hand
I will still be early for work
my nose is dripping
everyone is wearing winter coats, hats
and gloves
tomorrow it will be 60 degrees
and by Thursday all of NYC
will have a bad cold

The bus is slower at this hour of 8 AM
there is more traffic additional passengers
to stop for but it's different and I like
the change

people were found hacked to pieces
all over the place according
to the morning news
last night it was not a full moon
but it must have been something
perhaps a meteor shower in Hades

147

There is one man on the bus
he is wearing highly polished
black shoes
has his back hair combed up
over the top of his head
so even in that nice black suit
he looks ridiculous

I got myself a cyber lover
I know he is mashing on other girls
at the same time he is typing to me
Last night, he wasn't raunchy, so
I asked him why
I think
he was toning down his act
for me

I don't know how he looks
but I imagine he likes to comb
his back hair up over the top of his head
I imagine in person he is a drip

I imagine that his dripping exhibition
would include the wife and several kiddies
with clinging submissive women
lurking in the shadows
stalking him
he is my cyber lover
but if I ever meet him, he will have to
bow to domination
and put on a wig to cover that mess
coming up over the top of his head

148

Rainy fall day
leaves hanging on for dear life
knowing that to drop to the sidewalk
in NYC is not to rot into the earth
as nature intended

I have developed a new theory
on drug addiction, that junkies use
because they all have sensitive eyes
and shooting dope contracts
the pupils of their eyes to tiny pinpoints
not allowing the intake of excessive
burning light

They wear dark sunglasses
eat cheese doodles and drink orange soda
all well-known deterrents to a brilliant
atmosphere
their sensitivity also to the harsh
illumination of reality
that cuts them deeper than any
belt tied tight around their arm
and dope also closes the inner eye

stops it briefly from exposing
gruesome monsters and hideous replays
of yesterday's mistakes

That's my theory on the increasing
numbers of kids who have taken
to sticking needles in their veins and
powders up their nostrils
maybe it would be wise to
return to the simple farm life
where child labour and early death
could save us.

149

Another rainy day
we've had two in a row
but nice warm fall ones
and I don't care
I am safe and dry on #4316
the downtown bus heading into
another unknown devotion
my life dedicated to the hidden
possibilities of the future
the unfolding
the revelation of each new hour
my cyber boyfriend
did not appear last night
to mend my daily wounds
maybe busy or maybe punishing me
but Mr. Internet has called again
and I am trading a cyber fight
for a real live date
right after my therapist warned me
about indulging in dangerous fantasy

A younger Janet Whalen, a/k/a JD Rage
from a self-portrait color painting
converted to grayscale

I am happy for the moment
though my bad arm aches in the rain
and the bus is approaching work
where I must run the gauntlet
one more time before the weekend

150

On Veterans day it was announced
that possibly as high as 80% of
disabled Veterans are homeless
unable, after their stint of
guerrilla adventure in the Southeast
Asian jungles to ever live again
in comfort within the confines
of four walls
to accept and return to the
delicate sensibilities of gentile living
after learning
that it is all a lie
that death is the truth
and death does not come gentle to
the Third World

Death eats faces spotted with small black
holes from rapid fire weapons
swats down patriots regardless of
their national fervor
and brings young boys and girls with
shining faces from prosperous countries
to do the job for it
after reaching this degree of reality
a bed is beyond reason
a cardboard mat on Avenue A becomes
the only acceptable comfort
the side of a building for a bathroom

the bottom of a cheap pint to forget
no bus rides to a soft state job
no welfare checks for wine
and antipsychotic medications

151

Starting downtown from East 23rd Street
rather than Houston, it is later
the traffic is clotted
and the junkies are out
in their camouflage uniforms
with multiple piercings visible
above the neck
I feel good in my green nail polish
drugstore cowboy leather jacket
it is snowing

the sky winks a golden eye from gray
leopard patterns that rush across the
panoramic view from my bus window

College kids are walking to school
and I am wondering why Saturday's date
hasn't called me
St Mark's Church
presents a medieval vignette with its
old twisted trees
gnarled and leafless skeletons
against the backdrop of
dried out grass and stone walkways
finally the bus driver catches a break
and we glide all the way to east 4th Street
before hooking onto another snarl
of vehicles

As I see a cop writing out a ticket

and placing it beneath the windshield wiper
of a car, I remember walking down
St. Mark's Place on a Saturday night
with my date
me towering over him in 3 inch heels
listening to an ambulance with lights flashing
emitting its noise controlled screeches
The date smiled and told me
they don't have a true emergency
he knows these things
and carries a gun
he has handcuffs and a portable
red flashing light for his car
he will never bring that gun around me
he says

the bus has finally made it below Houston
where we have joined a flotilla of other buses
from here on we will ride together
and the waiting people will be asking
why do all the buses come at the same time

152

I'm sick today
upset stomach, messed up blood sugar
it's late but I am going to work anyway
all the passengers are speaking loud
Spanglish and Arabian
I wonder if all those who converse
in these languages are deaf
I have often heard those who can't hear
themselves raise the volume for that
reason
the sun is stunning, doing its
mid-morning romantic streak and ray thing

but it is cold, about 30 degrees
I am frozen

I have not seen one flower
they are all dead
it will be bare trees on their own
from here on in I fear
It would be nice if the Parks Department
planted some evergreens in Allen St. Park
around the fake gaslights
but they are probably afraid that such
a tree would provide to much
ground level concealment for
various criminal activities
the current maples and elms
do not sprout branches
until well above the height
of the average human

Bags of rice and powdered potatoes
are piled outside a delivery truck
near East Broadway
East Broadway itself displays a solid line
of white trucks parked on both sides
with occasional double parkers
also white trucks, obstructing the flow
of traffic
Chinatown sidewalks are congested
with shoppers
I survey every man who gets on
the bus for possibilities
they always fall short of my
lowest expectations
the playground is empty
one more stop to a warm office
and morning coffee

153

I don't think I can take it
my world is falling to pieces
the brusque tall Hispanic dispatcher
that I am in love with has not been
at my stop in over two weeks
my recent date is not going to call back
my would-be cyber master is angry because
I told him if he ever came near me
with a whip I would have to bash
his head in
I am sad that I have been reduced to this

work is around the corner
I am almost relieved to assume
my business persona
who is a straight determined workaholic
she can climb inside a stack of paper
and avoid contending with the dust

I have disintegrated into
dating perverts
dreaming of going to New Orleans
to be beaten and hung and smashed
into oblivion
the bus will not save me
the day smells of diesel fuel
and stale urine
but it is only my interpretation
of the circus on this one day
and nothing more

154

Outside the air is cool
water towers loom on the horizon

over the East River like castle turrets
a jet plane passes by silently
enveloped in a gray mist
two pigeons are silhouetted in front
of it on a rooftop
the craft is flying low enough
to appear as one of the flock
of seagulls wheeling over Houston Street
a punk rocker slouches at the
bus stop, not waiting for a bus, because
all of the various M's go by without
him boarding one, his connection
is not vehicular

Today I might receive a phone call
from the south
I do not want him to like me
but I am worried that he will not
he is into domination
but so am I
he would rule me when I could never
even control myself
he would flog me, suspend me
pierce me and draw blood
I suppose I would call this love

The Houston street gulls are far away
we have arrived at Worth Street and Centre
perhaps I should detour
to the 100 Centre Street Criminal Court
building and turn myself in
I may be in need
of a little protective custody.

There is a delay
the driver got off as we got on
I am in the back behind the barrier
near the wheelchair lift door
I feel him return to the command chair
and we start moving shortly thereafter
only a minute behind schedule

Someone told me the next time
I get on a bus, I should plant a bomb
but I prefer to reminisce about
the koi on my admirer's ass
a large black & white stylized beauty
(the koi - not the ass)
for which I would someday like to
go fishing, if he will return
the favor

Yesterday, I would have gladly
bombed this bus
with me on it
but now I have at least one week's
worth of curiosity to see what
developments will unfold
I am close to revealing my telephone
number which he has been working
his way around to for several weeks
playing me slowly
with great patience
for he feels the rewards will justify
the effort
so I will not plant any incendiary devices
today nor detonate any explosives
this bus is safe from execution
but I fear that I am not.

156

I think of a voice today
that I may never hear again
of a man who admires the image
he sees on a photograph
so much that he would like
to torture me

On the bus
a bumpy ride
is torture enough for me
and I recall other images of
women in bondage
clamped and bound and hung
with unspeakable bruises
covering them
inflicted it is said at their request
and for their pleasure

Finally I have found something
that truly revolts me and
of course, the more I am revolted
the more I am drawn in
but I have already been
tied and twisted up in the ultimate
form of bondage
of slavery to intoxication
chained to a syringe and a glassine bag
following them crawling and begging
on my bloody knees
No human sadist could ever top that

and so I think I will resist temptation
to venture toward that place within me again

157

The obsession has been broken
I have led my cyber dom
to reach his own conclusion
that I am fat and therefore
quite unworthy of his
mole-covered hairy attentions
I have sent him a copy of my book
with many references to confirm
his suspicion

I am sad at the speed of his flight
away from my spirit which travels
over the computer lines and phone lines
and airwaves

I loved the attention
playing him along
with protestations that I would never
be a slave for his harem
to make him want me more

I have been rescued by the force again
and I contemplate a lonely weekend
ahead from my blue seat
on this blue bus
that is made ever more blue
by seeing it through my sad
gray eyes

158

Thanksgiving is coming and I am
already hungry
but unfortunately I can eat nothing
or I will step a foot into my early

grave
This week I thought that living might
be the better alternative
now, once again I am not so sure
No food, No heroin, No cigarettes
No speed, No Jack D, No wine
No beer, No sex, No gravy
with all the No's
is there a Yes?
Oh plenty of yeses most assuredly
Yes loneliness, Yes desperation
Yes wrinkles, Yes insulin,
Yes grotesqueness is always on one's tail
the ayes have it you No
those yeses are a heartless killer
and can hardly be tolerated
without those shock-absorbing No's
to counteract depression
or maybe just to add to it
until it becomes sweet melancholy
but then I think of a smoke-filled
jazz club which brings me right back to
No cigarettes, No heroin, No Jack Daniels
so why do they call it Thanksgiving anyway?

159

Freezing my lovely face off
in the city where if you get upset
you throw your three children
off the roof
and then jump after
fall dead
and that will show them won't it?

I do know the feeling
try to contain it to my own body

and personal body parts

I sent my son away so he was quite safe
from insolent and infantile
retaliation methods
drugs I want to use drugs
there is a deal
early morning sales transaction
in the Allen Street Malls median strip
exchanges so obvious
but quick
buyers striking like hungry trout
and darting off into the weeds
or deeper waters
only three to four blocks
from the Methadone Clinic
Lower East Side Service Center
where they may go tomorrow if they
live out the day
and I would join them
and I would join them
what a laugh
I am no longer strong enough
for that kind of desperation
I can barely tolerate the easy life
with a roof over my head
and such a smooth bus ride today
I could barely tell that I was on one.

160

Yesterday
I did give thanks
and I remembered
Herbert Huncke and all the others
who will not suffer another holiday

cold has descended upon us again
it is frozen
like a stark February day
the tree are completely bare
which doesn't make much sense to me
in the winter

I want to wrap them up
in Grandma's quilts
but they would only be
stolen before sundown
there are people who need quilts
and people come before trees
because trees can not contend
with locomotion
they remain in bondage
for a lifetime
but they will undoubtedly
take their revenge passively,
by dying,
removing all their benefits
from the realm of our existence
where, though we will not
acknowledge it,
we depend on them
for almost everything

Grandma's quilts have long since
rotted away
and so, those trees are on their own,
I cannot save them

161

I am glad to be back
to my usual pattern
going on my morning bus ride

I have lost my timing
drop my knapsack on the floor
can't seem to get my pen out
until the driver calls "Delancey Street"

I am four pounds heavier
from a rich food business trip
I feel it as a pain in my gut
but I do look younger
a fattened face smoothes over
creeping old age wrinkles
when I think of them
they possess me
I am not gripped by them
when left alone
only when considering a
new opportunity for meeting
someone and preparing
once again to bare my scars
for inspection

when I view humanity as
a panorama from my bus window
we become insignificant
our wrinkles invisible
brush strokes hidden neatly
in the complexity of the
overall arrangement

162

miserable cold
the bitter rain compliments
my mood to perfection
the high winds
that flap the plastic sealing
dangerous construction areas

echo those that blow madly
inside my head
mimicking the high pitched
ringing in my ears
a residual from my years
of expressing rage
through pile driving accompanied
by my blaring music

fog is on the bus windows
fog is on my glasses
and clip on shades
blurry headlights
to the right
a patch of dark clarity
shines between the motion of
front windshield wipers

it is a good day to stay inside
all my fellow passengers
look like junkies
it is dress down Friday
could that be it?
more likely it is the unfortunate
fact that the Methadone
clinic does not make deliveries

163

Late and spitting nails
sick of bus driver power tripping
one waiting at the corner
while the sardine packed one
takes too long to leave the stop
and then inching up
making like he's going to

drive right by
herding us out into the middle
of the street with this maneuver
not opening the door
forcing us all back to the sidewalk
mouthing foul curse words
at the gloating dispatcher
and what can we do but
board sweetly
while wanting to yank the driver's ass
from behind the wheel and
smash him straight into
pancakehood
and then wash him down the sewer
tiny shreds of blue uniform
swirling in the putrid waters
of NYC

and now that I have said my piece
the driver can live
he has arrived downtown in
record-breaking time
rushing so he can have
his breakfast in the little
greasy spoon across
from City Hall

164

Crisp clear bright lovely cold
I'm not in pain, I'm right here
in the fourth seat of bus 8205
writing
people turn pages across the aisle
a woman reads a book in front of me
sunshine blinding from the left
as we pass the Williamsburg Bridge

on Delancey Street
trucks and cars breezing by at
the traffic light on Grand
kids and teenagers heading to school
I am on my way to work
two hours behind schedule
It's fine with me, I'm right here
as we join a long line of traffic
waiting to make the East Broadway light
writing
the first passenger gets ready to depart
my spine presses into the back
of the molded plastic seat
I read the Emergency Exit sign and
the words Kipling Safety on my knapsack
It will be a good day
because I'm right here experiencing it
deeply

165

Gray fast
speeding on Allen Street
has the blues
crowded bus waits at Delancey
picks up a lot of kids
going to school
it's always like this when
I'm late
but they are quiet children
and I rejoice
that the morning silence
will not be severely broken
Manhattan has a new torture
victim
a woman raped and covered

in hot wax by a man
she met on the internet
she went to his apartment
on their first date
a foolish idea from any point of view
I wonder if he told her about
his intentions
and she went anyway
loneliness can do that to a girl
or possibly to me
my netman makes no bones
about it - he would love to
cover me in hot wax
the one who just got arrested
was studying to be a scientist
at Columbia University
and nobody who knew him
would date him because he was
so weird
I wonder if wax causes any
lasting damage to one's skin

166

Woke up sick
head stuffed up
and ready to explode
I am off early
to the races
otherwise I will
not be off at all
last night, oblivion
took me early
a small mercy
to ease my suffering

out the window
are all the rain-slicked streets
and headlights
dawn is coming
creeping slowly in, possibly
as sick as I am
It will rain all day again
and lack of sun
will fuel the great
Christmas Depression
the suicide rate will go up
If I am lucky, a dose of
Alka Seltzer Cold Nighttime Plus
will make me sleep right
through it.

167

Dark depression
no sun for two days now
Vitamin D deprivation
no time for the news
don't know what horror
happened overnight
in my wild city
no one wants to live here
but I am happy enough
with the arrangement
unseen men with tattoos
and Prince Alberts call me sweet
over the airwaves
I wonder if that sends some
good Karma in my direction

Gold Star Auto School
is not open

large orange sacks of onions
are being unloaded
on the sidewalk providing
excellent contrast to a
storefront's gold and black sign
everything looks dull and dirty
Chinatown could use a
good cleaning
NYNEX pagoda telephones
advertise bagels in front
of King Wah Bakery
irony abounds as usual
I look down a side street and
catch a glimpse of the Brooklyn Bridge
off in the distance
I would like to be off in the distance
myself, a strong and silent
structure supporting the traveling
masses

168

Sweet warmth of the sun
makes one final appearance
before descending into winter's
frigid curtain where it will
not succeed in melting even
the first layer of ice
I have forced myself out
into it
the absolute cure for depression
I am still sick
I feel it within me
I feel the medication killing
all my bacteria
X-mas is upon me
many presents shy of this year's

requirement
I must shop after work
where the evening hovers like a
hungry vampire
waiting to suck me
dry

169

Sleep did not come easy
last night
now I sit within an
imitation cotton hangover head
though I was completely and horribly
alert until 4:15 AM
It is 8:05 now
wet spray under the umbrella day
SRO on the bus
heavy traffic as we reach Delancey
sometimes I feel
I cannot bear another day like this,
where upon rising I already
know that it will be inconvenient
from dawn till around midnight
with me yawning all the way
I would like to sleep
in my seat
but all my pills are brewing
in my stomach
every effort is directed
towards containing the vomit

the guy in the seat next to me
wants to get out
of course I have the laptop,
knapsack, book of devotions
and umbrella sticking

from my pocket
bile churns within
yet today in all this mess
somehow I know I am beautiful

170

Merry X-mas
from the deep I sing
riding to work
inside my still nauseous
body on Christmas Eve
Nothing looks different
it is warm
should be in the 40's
no major massacres
suicides or torturings
were discovered last night
although I am sure
they happened
probably right above
a group of joyous carolers
no big Christmas tree fires
nor celebrity deaths
have been reported
all is quiet
I am sicker than any dog
I have ever known
including Alex after
she ate the kitchen floor
dogs would always have the sense
to die before
they got this bad
I have purchased stupid
thoughtless
gifts
I have not put up my tree

or sent cards
or been able to hold my head
up in the air for five minutes
without gagging
my body always has defective timing
I feel like I used to
after shooting up some good heroin
but without the mitigating high
more punishment for my
crimes against humanity?

171

Red sky dawn silhouettes the
Williamsburg Bridge
backlit by the rising sun
a flock of pigeons circles the bus
as if we were a floating rooftop
and huge seagulls turn high
in the air above Allen Street
mutating this morning into a
beautiful omen

sleet and wet snow will begin tonight
the day after Christmas
whose exploding packages have put
some poor kid in the burn unit
there is no traffic
everyone is on vacation
we arrive early and head into
the stand of
gray downtown monoliths

172

Is my stomach to be
permanently queasy?
this flu drags on as I struggle
to work on 8188
fearing the act of sitting upright
from my slumping position
I dare to peek out the window
and the colored awnings
dingy trucks, pedestrians flying by
send me spinning
thank god this bus has
a good suspension

the driver speeds up
takes some bumps
causing my innards to churn again
in these final horrible days of
the year

we are going out
pallid limping invalids
bright sun notwithstanding

173

I think of the brevity of life
today, remembering now that
Lizzie passed a corpse last week
someone who had just been run over
by a bread delivery truck
that had backed up and crushed him
on Allen & Houston
close to the stop where I got on bus 4311
this morning

and how on the way home from
Christmas shopping I had experienced
the immediate aftermath
of a fatal car crash
on Clinton and Houston
people out for a Sunday drive
persons crossing the street
humans with a destination
and a purpose
maybe with someone awaiting
their arrival
a blink
an instantaneous whip flick
of time and this reality
is lost to all of them forever

this bus could be flattened
by debris from a falling airplane
any minute now
I listen for warning sounds from the sky

174

pollution
pollution
pollutioN
cold air dawn
fresh and calm
evaporates in a cloud
of second-hand cigarette smoke
compounded by a surge
of choking bus fumes
and black smog emitted from
the M&M garbage truck's
diesel exhaust

not as bad as the sidewalk level
bus effluvia,
but it definitely melts in
your lungs
not in your hands
red red sky
patrolled by gliding seagulls
portends of bad weather
before tomorrow

I sit across from a cute guy
in leather today
a silent cruel type of course
I can't look at him since he is
exactly my type
but I feel the companionship
of a possible fellow traveler
and try to send him mental waves
obscured somewhat
by a nagging headache
I want to tell him I have
immortalized him in this
poem today
but I will never even know
his name

175

I arrive at the bus stop
with my face frozen into
a protective mass
mentally I have willed my soft skin
into impervious stone
killing my ability to feel
this arctic wind blowing
over NYC's Lower East Side
with a fury best reserved for

ice storms at the barren South Pole

In my seat I am thawing
but in five minutes or less
I will be braving the wind tunnel
created by tall building
forces and anti-forces at
Federal Plaza
my world transforming
into a cubistic barrage of
competing angles
treacherous slicing diagonals
that I must navigate
like a super hero in order
to buy my morning coffee
at Blimpies on
Church Street

176

In storm time
I don't see the glow of
the red horizon that was
described by the weatherman
just a gray wash the color
of vile exhaust

pigeons feed en masse
at the tail end of the park
called Allen Street Mall
pecking up scattered rice
that has blended with
the sidewalk dinge
until the concrete itself
is a frantic smear of gray
everything is gray
everything is gray

except of course for the inside
of the bus driver's head
not this one who now maneuvers
9188 down to Chatham Square,
but the one who purposely
closed the door on me
after he saw me run across
lanes of oncoming traffic
to be on time for his bus line
certainly that driver's head
is devoid of any hint of
gray matter

177

very dark
all sun traces blotted out
by cloud cover
but still I wear my shades
especially in this bus
with its overbright fluorescents
blasting into my weary eyeballs
tonight I might play pool
for the first time in 12 years
with a kid from the internet
my current lover,
who is called slave

I am afraid
I hate going where people
can mock me
they will think my son
is treating me to a night in the
pool hall
even though he will be wearing
long red fake fingernails
as a handicap

and I will feel like
I did when my mother used
to force me to attend
the Friday night square dances
on Ellis Hollow Road
where I even mocked myself
all was ridicule and shame
that was me
now I have become a square dancer
not in the usual sense
I will not dance and
that makes me a square

downtown is in sight
work is here
to provide a slight diversion
from my madness

178

It is a very frigid day
but mercifully little wind
I feel warm
amazed at what the slight
attentions of a man
can do for me
I watch a seagull hover above
Houston Street
and I am up there with it

elation is exceeded only
by deflational
bubble bursting

well okay
just in case,
there is always the handsome

motorcycle man
who has taken to riding
the bus at the same time
as me
every morning

179

There is a new or temporary
fill-in dispatcher
I feel in love with him on sight
he is a big one
a Brooklyn accent wise guy
who wears a sweatshirt with
the hood up
on days with bad wind-chill factors
he is build like a fireplug
made to absorb the punishment
of long days outside
in cold weather
this is my third dispatcher affair

the other day, he allowed
the City Hall M-15 to take off
after slamming its door in my face
I guess that means the feeling
isn't mutual

real boys are asking me on pool dates
and to go out for coffee so I
may not have to settle for
my early morning bus stop
fantasies

I hear the new dispatcher tell
the hopeful waiting passengers
that he has lots of toys

no money he says, but lots of toys
it sounds like we may have
way too much
in common

180

my raging city is quiet
only the bus dispatcher is noisy
his laugh has a Brooklyn accent
too

It is currently one degree, but may
reach 30
it is darker than my soul
but still I attempt to remove
the fluorescent morning death rays
by wearing sunglasses

my motorcycle man is not
riding with us today
maybe he wimped out
or maybe he doesn't have
a warmer coat
today a motorcycle jacket would
freeze
crack into a million
particles
I wouldn't really mind breathing in
those little specks of leather
how much worse than our
regular NYC air can it be?

181

My essence is drenched
through and through
while waiting for bus 4306
in a steady cold rain

soaked and puddling rain gear
lines the aisles on the rubber floor
sending rivulets down the grooves

wet umbrellas and woolen gloves
do not work well together
nor do I and water of any type
my long leather coat
was no help at all

I feel like a sodden cat
I want to go home and curl up
on top of the bookcase

182

Even my bones are frozen after
waiting a long time on the
Allen Street tundra
waiting for the M-15
one foot has no feeling
it is the essence of zero and below
the pen is cold from exposure
inside my knapsack and
the ink is just now warming up
coming to life
on this page
which is also cool
to the touch
This is a good sign, I decide

it means my body temperature
is still high enough
to tell the difference
although my foot doesn't
feel the floor
only the solid core of itself
consumed into an icy blob

Outdoor workers are dressed
like Eskimos
only noses are visible out there
except for one guy
with bare blue fingers
smoking a cigarette

183

The cold is beginning to bore me
now that it is the only game
in town
everyday the same old thing
no new words to describe that
feeling of body systems slowing down
to become a block of ice
every morning the frigid trudge
to the bus
there is nothing to look at
but salt stained sidewalks

I imagine everyone else
snug in bed and me trekking
through below zero hell
alone
others are here with me
of course
but we don't really see each other
I shrink back into my two hoods

and multilayers
that most effectively cut off
my peripheral and frontal vision
and cause an extreme
lack of grace
but the wind has already struck
I am a skeleton without flesh
colder than death
with no earthly protection

the sun has begun to come up
shining in from the general
direction of Brooklyn
to shed some light on
this bleak day

184

The birds are out en masse
swooping and turning
flapping their wings in a dizzying
whirlpool above Houston Street
white fat seagull bodies
blanket the scene
I forget to be watchful of the danger
of falling bird droppings
in my fascination with the beauty
of this morning's flight

The weather has gone into a heat wave
it's 30 degrees
the forecaster says the ground
is sweating from the rapid change

I wish I could banish all bitter cold
from my vicinity
at least until my brain thaws out

They have ripped out the hedge
around the Federal Building
at Duane Street
a good bet that too many
suspicious packages were found
hidden beneath the greenery
the bare dirt looks lonely
but I guess it still must be
sweating

185

white tornado vacuum attack
to cacophony of major bird
squeaking and talking
fresh food fresh water
fresh food fresh water
squeak squeak squeak
shut up
shut up
squeak squeak squeak
sounds of neighbors
stirring in their beds
blasted awake by my extreme
lack of consideration
but slave is coming to get
his nails done tonight and
there is no other time to
rearrange my dirty life
no time to dust the visible surfaces
in the evening
I am excited
one can not avoid intimacy
with a man when affixing
fake fingernails
and applying red polish

as a handicap for pool
where I hope to win at least
one game
my claws will be trimmed short
and should for once
give me the advantage
I dream of my eight ball shot
sinking in triumph
on bus 4308
smooth as butter today
odd, since it's a full moon
and my head just exploded

186

Last night I glued false fingernails
on slave
polished them green
lost 7 straight games of pool
anyway
later played show and tell
with tattoos and piercings
He will be 25 one week after
I have 25 years on the job
hey I am still a viable human
people want to see my nipple ring
and I still want to show it
to them
I feel my steel
it is cold in the bus
this always brings an awareness
of the metal
my new friend has
a snake tattoo around his ankle
and can balance on one foot
for more than a minute

My best friend has nine years
clean and sober today
I rejoice under the brilliant
red morning sky
on display over the East River
as usual we will pay big for
this explosive exhibition of
glowing beauty
which is also the portent of
rotten weather on the way
who cares?
the elements can attack me
all they want
I am awakening after a
twelve year hibernation
and I have decided to feel
and so I want to feel everything
to take all life can spew
upon me and hope for more
there is a joy
in breathing
and dodging death
but with abandon
not solemnity
to play the game
not to watch it
that reminds me
I must pick up a new copy
of Willie Mosconi's book
on mastering pocket billiards
because I really want to know
how it feels
to win!!

This will be a
short ride
it is 7:05 AM
and raining
no traffic
no light
and it is warm
8 or 10 people
on the bus
quiet
except for
the usual bus
noises
shaking, revving
rattling
humming
brake pressure release
and we go around
the curve onto
East Broadway
on the tail of the South Ferry
bus through Chinatown
past a few
early rising store owners
putting out their stock of
vegetables, fruit or fish
in the dark
we cruise though
the intersection
and here we are
Federal Plaza 7:11 AM
6 hot minutes
what a ride

J.D. RAGE READS POETRY
AT ABC NO RIO 157 RIVINGTON ST.
3:30PM
SUNDAY 7/23/89
ALSO OPEN READING

Daylight
half moon
hangs over Delancey
in clear but
gray tinged
blue sky
puffy cellulite clouds
below
no red at all in this
morning vignette
but cold again
I don't much feel it
my brain warm with thoughts
of a certain live body

There is a fire blockage
announced on East Broadway
we detour to Madison Street
dark tenement buildings
surround us instead of
Chinatown's usual
shopping atmosphere
I and the passengers crane our necks
wondering if we can tell
what is burning

190

A chill portrait
of impending snow
drills into my head
but --
I am on a rollercoaster

one thing tumbling by
after another
dates, tattoo appointments,
visions of horses with fiery manes
coming to life on my back
pool games with men wearing
fake red fingernails
anniversary of the day Sid died
2/2/79
my clean date 2/7/85
dedicated lines, cell phones
moving into high tech life
hours on the internet
creating a magazine
issue #7 -- a lucky number
if ever there was one

191

Last day of January
I feel like this should be
New Years Eve
big date tonight
someone is going to want to hold me
to run his red fingernails
through my hair and
tell me I am beautiful
In order to be able to allow this,

I have booked an appointment for pain
to begin a major tattoo
I am hoping this invasive procedure
can counteract
my excessive brain power
that is already trying to
twist/blow up/blow out/
smash/desecrate

and annihilate my small good fortune

I will have Anil
the tattoo master to parry
the attempted destruction with beauty
to confront my spending mania
with huge hourly fees

the bus dispatcher was exercising
this morning
I stood very close as he stepped
up onto the curb and back down off it
20 times a minute
until he cornered a passerby
and told her his whole life story
with exaggeratedly loud voice
he is going to Florida tonight
with his girlfriend to visit his daddy
It will take him 2 1/2 hours to reach
Maryland
I am going on my own little trip
tonight
but I will not have to leave OZ

192

Why is it that when one thing
goes right everything else must disintegrate
this world must dissolve into miserable ashes
There was sex with a beautiful boy
but then BOOM! canceled tattoo appointment
no phone and no computer
entombed in the loneliness
that I have only recently broken away from

In three days I will have twelve
years clean and sober

and no one can even call me
I can't speak with my new young lover
it's time for a cell phone
I think as I sit on this bus in the rain
this bus that was one half hour late
on the day when I am carrying a
laptop, a knapsack and an umbrella
But still I am grateful
to be sitting
hopeful that the tension
in my neck will dissipate quickly
hopeful that the agitation I feel
after screaming at poor birdie Nero
to shut up! shut up! shut the FUCK UP!!!
and scaring him, my tiny parrot who
is already announcing with screeches
that he is unhappy just like me
hopeful that my brain's
spin cycle will soon end

I am not screeching
but my insides have gone totally
BERSERK and little Nero was
probably only doing my screeching for me
work is ahead, I will suffer its
indignities gladly today
since there I will have a telephone
and no longer be cut off
from the world

193

The MTA seems so dependable now
at least the bus comes everyday
even if mostly not on time
or packed to the gills

or manned by nasty drivers
The MTA, compared to NYNEX
is a shining angel
is as constant as a rock

NYNEX has been pulling my chain
jerking me around
screwing me over
and pissing me off
for three days
no phone service
no computer modem service
and they tell me lies
they tell me the repair guy was there
they tell me he fixed it
they tell me he left a card
they fixed it from the central office
and did not need to pay a personal visit
but he was not there and didn't fix it
and left no card and the central office
says "I still show trouble on the line"
The trouble with my line is NYNEX
today I will demand a supervisor
a more expert liar and tomorrow
I may pay a visit in person

Now I am on the bus
dreaming of slave,
who called me beautiful last night
and almost erased my NYNEX nausea
the bus is jerky and bumpy today
I think of the solitary gull
I saw patrolling the mottled blue gray sky
over Allen Street and wait for the
extra strength Advil to take effect.

The bus driver gives me
a pleasant half smile
I return it as the other half
together we have created
a complete grin

my back is stinging
but in a singing way
the new horse whose name
is RAGE
rears up his hooves
slashing
and flares his tail
lightning bolts and flames
adorn his mane
he is my protector
a replication of the inside
of my soul
where also live a black horse
named 13 and a white horse
called Exit
with manes of green snakes
and purple feathers
guarding me or composing me
or reconstructing me

the bus is surrounded
by low flying gulls
swooping in to take food
from the sidewalks
with the pigeons
of East Broadway

It is an extreme vision as
the driver carefully maneuvers

through them
I am happy and
the bus has reached my destination

195

This bone chilling weather
requires no wind-chill factor
to make me feel
as if my skeleton
were carved of ice
merciful fate
sends a bus quickly today
my new tattoo is itching
badly forcing me to hold
my back unnaturally away from the
hard plastic seat
I am a mess
infatuation always does this to me
I am in The Last Picture Show
I am the coach's wife
but without the coach
and without the handsome
high school boy

the lid of my metal box
has been pried up
my overflowing heart contents
have amassed beneath in
swirling radioactive ribbons
ready to leap out and cause
a lot of chemical burning
the cover is cracked
I cannot seem to push it back
into its former
hermetically sealed position
I want to eliminate everyone

my college boy lover
is only here to learn a thing or two
and is in line for suffocation
everybody on this bus will be smothered
so I do not have to expose
my humiliation before them

the dispatcher, my imaginary mad love
now back from cheating on me with
his wife on their Florida vacation
steps up and down the curb
off the sidewalk
on the sidewalk
up and down up and down
reminds me that I am going
to Florida soon myself
I can let this mess of love stuff
go onto my parent who will
probably not even notice

I am cold now
an open wound in this world.

196

another cold one
I notice changes below Houston
Zaren Fabric Warehouse
has spruced itself up -
can this mean a resurgence?
will all these dingy crumbling
buildings be painted and
gentrified with
beautiful black satin signs
covering the closed off windows
of 2nd floor storage areas?

down on East Broadway
everything remains the same
this bus is wasting no time
my back is itching like mad
tonight I will sit for
two more hours of tattoo ink
the first two didn't hurt
with what I have been through,
I am way beyond such minor pain

the courthouses all look clean
and imposing

from inside the bus,
there is no clue of the
biting winds

197

I am in a strange mood today
there are three horses on my back
where yesterday was one
and just a week ago was
virgin territory

every bag of garbage, black hefty bags
ripped open and spilling out
squashed rotten onions
with entwined remnants of their orange netting
reminds me of a dead animal
in the street
which I approach praying
it will not be
but more than half of me
hoping it will
so I can see the twisted mass

of guts and bone
the dead dog face
so tragically blinded in oblivion

a white plastic bag
seems to me the body
of a cat or small dog
or large seagull
until it floats away
carried in the suction of
an approaching truck
just before going under
the wheels
I want to view a disaster
to be swept away
consumed by violent emotions

a number has been scrawled
on the back door window
of this bus 8469
I wonder if I should play it

198

The sidewalks are white
with the dryness of winter
today they will be covered
with salt again
to await tomorrow's
sleet storm
hopefully this will be
our last

we may have a lying
groundhog
as arctic weather has
arrived in force

immediately after two of them
predicted an early spring
in Long Island the little beastie
claimed to see its shadow
as the groundhog day celebration
has become
only one more thing
on which to make a buck
so now we have dueling predictions
as if any of these mayors
or other political types
who claim to be interpreting
for them would have
a chance in Hell of comprehending
the simplest thoughts of
this superior creature
from within their slime infested
brain cases
otherwise as empty as if
after a visit to the lobotomy
laboratory

199

St. Valentine's Day 1997
3 years before
the turn of the Century
12 years after my resurrection
I have a date
with a sweet young boy
this bus is so romantic
these puddles of icy slush
around my feet
take on the shape of cupid
drawing his bow
not even the weather can cheat me
there will be sultry sex with him

so much better for
his heavy heavy metal
in the right places
I will give him a ruby earring
so small it will add only
one tiny speck of color
perhaps the sight of it
in twenty years will cause him
to remember
his older woman
her valentine gift
and her tattoos
as I hope to fondly
remember him

the wipers swing back and forth
the driver is handsome
the dispatcher is also gorgeous
but nobody looks that good
to me today
because I have my own
I have my own
God bless me

200

My days as a Mistress
will be limited I'm afraid
My young friend wishes me
to tie him up and beat him
but does not want to be my slave
he has a Mistress, Lady Death
a woman he has never met
so I find myself playing
second fiddle to nothing
an entirely unenviable
position I realize

he wishes to be a friend
who also shares sex
but now there are
other things I must consider
since he seems so willing
and even eager to go it unprotected
with someone who says
she is a junkie (me)
it makes me wonder where
else he might have been
this naive child who could
easily kill me with his ignorance

All this venturing from my cave
feels a lot like Russian Roulette
crack the whip, take a spin
the trigger will pull itself

I want to lash him with a horsehair whip
and bind his legs and arms
with black leather ribbons
I want to pierce his private parts
with yet another metallic bar
I must not sink to despair
the future can never be carved
in stone because it has not
yet happened

201

Only 2 people on this bus
and one is the driver
the dispatcher's voice too loud
for my early morning ears
which have heard nothing but

monotonous low-volumed bad news
3 people now, another passenger
ascends at Houston Street before
departure

Fatality
someone has been struck and killed
while changing a tire on
one of the expressways
how many others have died during
the night?
how many ghosts are out there
frolicking among the whirling
seagulls

On my back
a pure black horse has made
his full appearance
he will declare his
presence painfully
for a brief but intense time
before completely melding
with my skin in order
to protect me
his mane is a clot of writhing
snakes
I have seen him before
rearing up angrily inside of me
now he appears quite placid
but he is life itself
the middle horse is Rage
the white horse to the right
of my spine is
death exit
exit death
a portent of the future
but also further protection
from it

my inked reapers lording
it over all
a white reaper above the black horse
a black reaper above the white
a reaper in Native American
headdress
brandishes his war stick
above the flailing hooves
of the wild red stallion
everything is in harmony
all is completely balanced
that is my essence

202

At the bus stop
I survey each passenger
and passerby with an eye
toward beating them
heavily about the back
and thighs with a whip
wondering if
I can really do it
and if I could get
a few volunteers for
testing purposes
but these men simply
read the paper
or stare blankly out into space
while I continue
in my sadistic fantasies
I have become a hedonist
a pleasure hound
and will seek its excesses
anywhere it wishes to be found

As the bus brakes jar me
without mercy I plan
a trip to the hardware store
for chains, locks, flyswatter
clothesline rope, silver tape,
plastic clamps
and a visit to the S&M supply house
for leather restraints and
a suitable collar
It won't go to waste
I can use it to dress myself up or as useful
items to have around the house

In my ramblings
at the stop
I envisioned
severe corporeal punishment
for a prospective casualty
a short chubby black man
in dungarees
and round blue sunglasses

He was crossing Allen Street
and suddenly,
while still captured in my gaze
he ripped his leg on a jagged
fence as he attempted
to skirt the median divider
he let out a loud yelp
that now echoes in my head
causing me to wonder
if the universe has been
reading my mind
again

Enveloping grayness dulls the view
but there many interesting items
on the sidewalk
a shrink-wrapped booklet called:
"How to Use a Condom"
a pair of lime green socks
a packet of Easywider rolling paper
a crushed Deer Mountain spring water
non-bio degradable plastic
container

the bus is quiet
light ridership on a Friday morning
I am dressed down
my black is flaking as the
scraped skin of my tattoo
the black horse 13
falls off in scaly sheets
to reveal underneath
a horse more intense than
Black Beauty
or Black Gold
the Triple Crown Winner
the horse representing all
that is dark within
the horse who has felt the sting
of life's training crop
and who has fallen repeatedly
when taking the high jumps

the bus jerks and bumps
bad brakes once again
and I wonder if the City
can really be this quiet
or if it is just less raucous

than the constant ringing
inside my own head

204

With my sunshine blinders on
I am riding by the February trees
still bare with seed balls hanging
in skeleton branches like tarnished
Christmas ornaments
I imagine the green thoughts
building within them
trying to erupt
their soft presence
through hard exterior matter
there are no complications today
life is serene
is bright and spotless
even the car that turned
on its back on the Queens Expressway
has been uprighted
and the passengers
are unharmed
I hope this will continue
to play out as one of the ten best days
even though I am sure my boss
will use his lack of knowledge
and his thinly disguised S&M techniques
to destroy it
the bus has arrived on East Broadway
we are going slow today
moving at the same speed as
the rhythm of my blood.

Almost froze my face off
trudging to the bus stop
my ears may have frostbite
but I am still overdressed
no good seats left
lots of standees
everyone rides on a cold day
I am ice
I have been cubed
I could easily shatter
or be harvested from the apartment
roof gutter like an icicle
all the air is beautiful
proving once again
again again again
that beauty is cruel
or that without cruelty
beauty cannot exist
a mad Palestinian shot down
some tourists at the
Empire State Building Observation deck
and then blew himself away
citing hatred for French, English
and American governments
I can't help but wonder
why he killed a Swedish musician and
a boy from Finland
and injured an Hispanic guy
from the Bronx
among the six caught by his revenge
he could have just shot himself
first, but maybe he was worried
that with only one death
and that a suicide
it wouldn't make the papers
that of course is a very valid concern

myself, I feel so jaded that
I commented "Only two deaths, well that's
nothing"
and I am sure that in this assessment
I was not alone

206

"We Buy All Junk Trucks"
reads a large sign on a passing
vehicle
Everything seems bad
already its is a junk truck of a day

traffic sucks
I let one bus go because if I
wanted to stand, I would have
caught the subway
the next one takes an eon to appear
the dispatcher is not restlessly
doing sidewalk Stairmaster
as usual
but is standing sedately
making lots of notes on his log sheets
I finally get a good look at his face
and I see he isn't really handsome
must reality always be so extensively
disappointing?
so brutally realistic?
his face is flat
features too small
eyes beady
I hope I can return to
the illusion combination
Brando/Stallone dispatcher
of my imagination
I have successfully countered reality

before but it is getting
more difficult
I worry
nothing is to be taken for granted
nothing is carved in stone
and something always turns into nothing
nothing is our destination I know
but can't we have a little fun
on the way?

207

Uneventful walk to Allen Street
the ringing inside my head is quiet
like a gentle surf
it threatens to rain
so I have worn my cute leather hat
It is 50, but feels hotter
and may reach 70
I leave for Florida on Saturday
had dreamed of escaping
the frozen North
but it will be warm everywhere
I hope there are no major
air disasters today or Friday
I want to sleep on the plane
all the way to Atlanta
but will not if freshly inspired
by the frenzy of a new explosion
disintegration or conflagration
I have recently proclaimed
my desire to live
there are now things to
exist/suffer for
there are feelings to be conquered or
negotiated

excitement fills me and spills over
the sides of my container
eating holes in my surroundings
like a corrosive chemical spill
I want to burn and dance and feel the pain
and even love
but I do not want to do all this
in a single split second on the
Delta flight to Dothan Alabama

208

Yesterday I applied
long blood red nails to
my own fingers
and today
writing on this bus
I am an exotic creature
riding here
riding with my face
soaked in cell regeneration
cream
my body starved and yet
still my stomach remains
my own personal
portrait of Dorian Gray
boy, did Oscar Wilde know
what he was talking about!

I think of Nancy Spungeon
dead for many years and of
the night I met a woman
who knew one of the doctors
present at her autopsy
I think of this for too much
will always be revealed

and revelation will
sometimes cleverly conceal
the romance of a situation

This doctor told the woman
Nancy had the organs of
a seventy-year -old woman
everything dissipating
and decaying rapidly
due to extreme neglect and
willful over saturation
but Nancy never had to face
up with it like I do

My surgeon informed me
my tissues are like toilet paper
which is why
the inside of my stomach
now has a screen in place
to keep my abdominal contents
from spilling out again
that must be quite a picture
on the outside, however, is
the real portrait
grinning and winking
with ribboned stretchmarks
and artificial surgical smiles
all of it tending to sag
over my privates.
when I look I am never
tempted to smile back

That being the case
I guess I might as well
get those privates pierced today.

There is a bad hair day
going on outside my window
caused by rain this time
not wind

I am of the Wind Clan
therefore the landing
of Delta Jet 7109
at Newark Airport
in high winds was successful
however, even though
I could save myself
with these royal connections
I could do nothing about
the four young girls in Queens
who were crushed
when the van they were sitting in
was demolished by a falling tree
its roots exposed by careless
construction
we are all to blame for that
always protecting our own roots
but caring little for the things
to which we owe
our lives
its roots made weak
by unauthorized digging
a high wind of 70 mph,
still 20 mph slower than a
good pitcher's fast ball,
took the tree and put it down
on a school van
killing 4 passengers
young girls all of them
but
I am still kicking

who can ever fathom the
decisions from beyond
it was time for them to go
and the wind took them
I merely experienced
a rough landing in Newark
all the passengers applauded the pilot
on touchdown
all of them but me.
I was too busy crying.

210

If you look at the number 20
from the back
through a window on which
it has been engraved
it looks like OZ, really
OZ with a backward Z
but then that is what OZ is
all about
backward and upside-down
reverse and mirror images
seen through
sparkly red sunglasses
twiddle dee
plays the wizard
and the song
If I Only Had A Heart
blares across a field
of waving poppies
of dreams
and night visions
monstrosities
multiple personalities
abominations
walking tin cans

talking piles of straw
like me
something inside is
walking my
bones
covered as they are in
a pliable flesh shell
and harboring some kind
of throbbing pit
some dangerously
empty tank
running on fumes
of the past

will I be able to
keep up this charade
for one more day?
for one more bus ride?
that is always the question.

I live in OZ
with a backward Z
that is me.

211

It is time
for warmth to return
I have run out of exciting ways
to say cold
and yet today the wind
hurt my face again
I guess trying to preserve me
by a non-voluntary
ambulatory cryogenics
procedure

The trees have not yet
got the primal message
to bleed green from their
abundance of fingertips
to dress up for the
balmy months ahead
to melt into lovely
waving landscape
enhancers

Everything is cockeyed
so don't be surprised if the trees
try to grow wheels
and mutate into
conveyances for human
children
I have recently been told
that the squirrels in
Tompkins Square Park
have taken to hiding
their gathered nuts in temporarily
empty baby carriages

212

Not being Friday the 13th
but merely Thursday the 13th,
it is not my lucky day
I am well rested
went to sleep at 8 PM
finally winding down all my
frenzied avoidance patterns

my father is more of a mess
than me

three strokes
left him with double vision
shaky hands and
poor balance
all of the things I took drugs
to achieve and the pursuit
of which left me in
sad physical condition

Dad just turned 79
he doesn't know me
as far as who I really am
although he recognizes my face
I don't know him either
and he will be gone soon
and though no one can ever
be sure about the enigma of fate
it appears I will outlive him
allowing me to suffer
one more psychic scar.

Can I take one more hit
I wonder because I have
had enough
my father is superman
he can't die
but then look at superman
the men who played him
one of them was a suicide
another died a vegetable
I would refuse the role
if I were an actor
even though
I sometimes seriously consider
resigning from my current
acting assignment.

If I were a wet cat
I would not be going
to work today
right now the idea
of huddling in a doorway
or an alley
with soaked fur
is more appealing
than this bus ride to City Hall
where I am damp
the wipers are going
the man next to me
is inconsiderate enough
to make me bend sideways
to fit my ass in the seat
people are coughing
spasmodically
noses are dripping
for all I know
other genital piercings may be itching
the man on the other side of me
is twitching
he has one of those
perpetual motion conditions
most likely brought on
by high doses of psychiatric medication
but I don't really care
sitting in this position
is stretching the tight nerve
in my back
finally! a seat!
but I am still not happy
soggy cold uncomfortable
on my way to work

those damn wet cats
have it made, not to mention
those wet vagrants and all the dry
independently wealthy
who did not have to leave
their warm condos today

214

It is Monday morning
the first day of my latest
depression
I can feel the endings
of my senses dulling
as they reach to strangle
my brain and my throat

scenery passes, that never stops
but it is all blank
I can't be bothered
to differentiate between
the levels of dinge
on all the white delivery trucks
today
it is my decision
I could be cheerful
I could start the day over
but I don't want to
this is a good place to begin
a self-indulgent bout with misery

my heart is still well surrounded
with solid steel barriers
only a few niches of light
require sealing
this can be accomplished

in under an hour
and so I will not need
to buy that jackhammer
after all, I can crawl
back into my soft velvet coffin
and learn again to accept the silence

fun is never as fun as
it is cracked up to be
when the fun is over
it is good and goddamn over
leaving only several more
irritating memories to eradicate

215

refreshed after three days
of adrenaline agitation
I sit on the late bus to City Hall
I fell asleep early on my couch
last night and didn't wake
until morning
dreamless sleep is the purest form
of escape
next to death

I have been praying for it again
for death
praying for a tall building
to fall on my head
for the sidewalk to sink
from beneath me dropping
my carcass into oblivion

praying for a bullet or a knife
to pierce me and allow

my trapped life force
to exit from this human cage
for a car to mash me into
the pavement
to return all this inconvenience
to a bloody but logical
pile of cartilage, veins and bone

I have been at the advils again
my new form of valium
they calm me
put me into a drugged stupor
and sometimes even make
my separated shoulder
stop hurting

216

my insanity is on the rampage
raging, making me again certain
I have chosen the right name

I am up at the crack of dawn
when even the crack of dawn
is not up
I can't sleep or settle
those mental molecules
into any sympathetic order

I want to kill someone
kill
I want to kill something
grab it by the neck and squeeze
the life out of it

maybe I will feel better then
if I can suck in that foreign energy

that freshly released vapor of life
as it vacates my victim's body
to steal it for myself
to capture the extra essence
I seem to require
in order to deal with anything

But do these bus passengers
around me look like prospects?
Nah - hell they all
look much worse than me
kill one of them
or even the sullen driver
and I would soon find myself
checking into the nearest
asylum for a quick lobotomy.

217

The old tattooed lady
has triumphed once again
placing herself on display
and throwing down
all of herself to the floor
of the lion's cage for adulation
and desecration
bathed in accolades
in praise and ripped within
the treacherous jaws
of a roaring beast
once again
home to the empty kitchen
the barren bedroom
the sad computer screen
home to no one
to the emptiness
made all the more vacant

by the expulsion of all the essences
and the presence of nobody
who can remember
what used to be inside

with her all that is remembered
is the outside
the pretty colors
of grim reapers
skulls and wild horses

the bus is a jerky one
the old tattooed lady's hand
lurches across the page

218

the lie of laughter is dying out
and the bleak settles in
more like real
more like my familiar circle
I gave up with a fight
the adrenaline push
the pacing nights
the pathetic longing
the leakage of faith
the constant knowledge
that another error has been made

next time and
I will make there be a next time
even though destined to always be
more painful than the most recently
departed attempt to connect
next time I will not engage
in negative speculation

if my suspicions are true
so what
it only makes me a brilliant reject
as opposed to an ignorant one
I still seek the bliss
I have heard so much about
I will apply my brilliance
to the pursuit of shining and sparkling
I will shine and sparkle to outdo
the brightest supernova
I will be even more intense
not less
I will defy the odds again
my own odds that always cast me
as a long shot on the rail
I may break a leg
and flop my way to a crashing collapse
I may have to be put down
If so, I say a gun applied
to the brain properly can
give relief better than
almost anything

219

soggy standing bus ride
lucked out into a seat
in the back row
neck hurts from lugging
new Powerbook computer
tattoo tonight
Anil will color in
my wild horses
and put snakes in their manes
I am to remind him to inscribe
their names

XIII and Exit
spring is here
even though cold as a dead fish
and wet
I feel it rumbling
under the cement in
the Allen Street Park
in the trees
and in the small patches of grass
I can see from my kitchen window
the cats have begun to yowl
in the night
I feel it in myself
I wonder if this year
spring's desire to mate
will again go unrequited

220

Late inking session
left me
with a good
but short night's sleep
floating on endorphin release
fantasy calmness
combined with
cool healing light
sent by a new friend
from the country
an upstate internet acquaintance
who says
I don't realize my own value
and asks if I know how much
he is amazed by me
what do I know?

I know nothing
so what do I know?
only that I am on bus 8489
running on four hours sleep
heading into
another fray

221

This Good Friday isn't so bad
the bus came quick
the weather is pleasing
the tattoo is healing
I don't care about anything
today
I have stopped myself
from thinking
I have placed a blinding fireball
in my brain
that obscures all messages
from the heart or loins

In 2 seconds we arrive
at Grand Street
the green awning of the
Grand Street Home Center
marks the trail
I am still okay
slept well for a change
and I personally
will not be hanging on a cross
today
or waiting for a spaceship
on the outer fringes of
the outer limits

Ptr Kozlowski and JD Rage at CBGB's in 1983
photo by Karen Williams

like the alcohol and phenobarb
Heaven's Gate crew
who have taken life
in hopes of immortality
in hopes of escaping
a planet slated for destruction
or in hopes of just not having
to think for themselves
with their too genius brains
anymore
I think I know what that feels like
but I prefer the Gates of Hell
and I will simply stay put
since I am already here.

222

Extreme body modification
was discovered on the
Heavensgate corpses
mods so severe
that there was nothing
left in which to insert
a prince's wand
castration is a very radical choice
but I understand that sex changes
male to female can retain
orgasmic capability
when female to male surgery
can usually not preserve
it
an old Greek eunuch
when asked
said women experience
nine or ten times the pleasure

that men do
I believe it

removing the penis
alone is not enough to transform
a man to woman
and so retaining is not the same
as gaining

knowing this
it would be silly for
a woman to attempt the change
if pleasure was her goal
I don't claim to know a lot about it
but to me body modification
piercing tattooing
scarification
branding
is the stuff of ancient ritual
and I was not shocked by the
condition of the bodies
awaiting the arrival of that ghostly
rescue spaceship
what I do know is
that getting pierced
exactly where I am
can make a rough bus ride feel
pretty damn good

223

April snow
wet icy crusts over
tender shoots of new grass
wondering if it is
worth the trouble
to push itself up through

last year's dried up brush
the cherry blossoms
shiver in hard winds
my hands frozen
my ears thawing
back seat of the bus
of course
with leaking window
feet cramped up
on top of back wheel
upstate is buried in white
schools are closed
Mass is in a state of emergency
I look at a man's
freshly shaved bald dome
and wonder if he is a skinhead
when not at work
and if he has clandestine piercings
and if like my ears
his head is warming up
the gas station flags
stand perfectly horizontal
as if starched and backed
with cardboard,
held that way by the
unrelenting wind

After all, it is April Fool's
and this is the first joke
of the day

224

The clocks have
all been turned back
I am surprised to be up early
ordinarily the time change causes

a major disruption in my normal
flow of energy
but this year I have a new itchy
back tattoo to get me out of bed
and a 2 and 1/2 day old pierced tongue
to arouse me from my sleep

I am in love with myself
losing weight
off of insulin
looking better than good
I am hot stuff
soon to cross the half century mark
I am aging like expensive wine
maybe partially due to long term
saturation with any and all of the finest
and cheapest of alcoholic spirits
I feel preserved in some way
the fall, the descent
from romantic infatuation
with the desire to be only
and always striving for a glimpse
at the world through the bottom
of a bottle or a sight of
the blood rising in ribbons
in the plastic syringe
the decline and exile from
intoxicated grace brought me
to my angel
delivered me up naked
into its care
where I am now being led
into another type of
eternity

It is nearing spring
but I am frozen solid
after waiting 20 minutes
at the bus stop
in the cold wind
the sunlight looks warm
but it isn't
nothing around me
is warm now
people for whom
I have performed
Herculean tasks
ignore my presence
of course I knew
it was going to happen
seeing a man who disintegrates
at every new level of
intimacy
he is not the one for me
too young, completely passive
submissive
an "I have no choice" kinda guy
I don't mind being ignored
I know its part of the game
he will come back
for I have stored the hair
I shaved from him
in a magic bowl
I know I said I wouldn't
do that again
but it was a spell
too available to pass up
casting
I will be flushing
the curly mess anyway
because I also know that

one day soon
I will not welcome his return

226

I arrive at Allen Street
with a thick scarf
wrapped around my face
too cold to notice anything
but the wind

It is time for me to move on
from my internet fantasies for
those who once were brilliant
have turned into dreadful
tarnished bores

all the fish in that sea
are as damaged as I once was
with ripped scales
rotting meat
foamy white mouths
grey clouded eyes
they do not swim free and so
become stagnant from
doing their endless rotations
inside small glass bowls
fouled with their own excrement

I need to find another sea
from which to dredge up
my one true love
my own gills
have been restored to health
and I wish to swim
among similar company

My friend Regan is dead
in Chicago
apparently there were
gory details
but then Regan wouldn't
have it any other way

I am still alive again
another younger one
has been shown the last exit
before me
I hope her suffering is over
because mine is not
I am in the agony of loss
Regan, Steve, Steel and all the rest
I miss you
I am not going to pretend
I was your great friend
because I am deficient
at communing with the living
but I will keep you in my
dark heart
because you have not disappointed me
have not ever attempted to discard me
though I have tried to escape
from your living forms
more than once
as the fear
choked its constant fingers
around my neck

Regan is dead
in Chicago

as one more chunk of beauty
is removed and starts its fading
into black

228

I am sick again
nausea and sour stomach
better than yesterday's deep pain
in every bone
everything is part of an endless
repetition of everything else
couldn't something be different
couldn't this bus ride be filled
with angelic choruses
couldn't my body resist
the plunge
couldn't one man be constant,
enlightened, loyal
and couldn't just one guy
be what he appears to be?

yes, the bright sun streaks
in the bus window again
the shadow of my pen on the page
highlighted in its streaked wash
yes, East Broadway is lined
with graffitied white delivery trucks again
and the people scurry like ants
to jobs or shopping
the same as always
except more because I am late today
but even that is the same
I am late each year
after daylight savings
until my inner rhythms adjust

to outside artificial changes
a change that occurs the same way
every year
and now we round the turn
onto Worth Street again where
the court buildings loom on all sides
as they have done daily
for ten decades or more
and the Asian seniors exercise
in the playground
the people wait in long lines
for driver's licenses
and me -- I am here again too
nothing is different
even the handsome goateed man
with the black beret who rides
in the front of the bus
will leave without saying a word to me
as usual

229

Paranoid today
the people all seem to be
peeking over my shoulder
looking at the red skin
on my lip where I have failed
at a waxing experiment
observing my clandestine secretiveness
knowing I have a metal barbell
in my tongue
watching me try to deal in a gentile
manner with my clogged-up
left nostril
instinctively going for this wounded
creature's throat

my back tattoo
is very slow in healing
the snakes are being recalcitrant
refusing to writhe their way
into my skin
puffing and arching and cracking
my surfaces
the feathers are also refusing
to unruffle themselves
their bluish purple tinge
not settling easily
the tail of the red horse
the final touch
will not cease its flicking
the strands of horsehair as
course as the real stuff
but they must subside and join me
these elements of protection
I will ask a magickal friend
to send me some healing energy today
he sometimes baby-sits
for polo ponies
he knows how to handle
a horse

230

I think if you have
a good date
with fun and laughter
lively discussion
pleasant waitress
well prepared food
that means you will

probably never see
her again
that means he was
not uncomfortable
he was not squirming
in his seat
he was not excited
and if he tells
you things you never
thought you would
hear
great things are in store
for you
or I will help you
find a publisher
or I am glad we
did this
you may be right
you will never
hear these things
because he was
only trying to please
you
and if he pays for
dinner that is
this kiss of death
done to hide his
guilt
at making a
spectacular pursuit
which he now
intends to
turn off like a
rushing faucet
and return to
the vacuum void

I must remember
to buy some locks today –
you would think
with all the locks
I have, there would
be enough
but they are the wrong
size and do not
fit through the
security devices
on the new leather
hand restraints
or leg restraints
then there must
be a chain
going from neck
to hands and hands
to feet or he
will be able to unlock
himself –
he does not wish to
have a choice
he wants to be
coerced by a
monstress
he wants to be
helpless and unable
to escape
to release the pressures
of his young life
to me
and he wants to
feel some pain
could drip hot wax

on him in very
tender places
could whip him
until welts build
but unfortunately
I do not think
he is worth it –

232

Sunglasses have
been purchased
for the summer
everyone is wearing
theirs today
now they all look
like me and I am
invisible my
eyes water
in the bright glare
above the East River
as the golden
orb rises on
our horizon
No, the glasses
are not dark enough
for this pool –
playing movie goer
always yearning
for the dark
who had fun
in the night
with her boy toy
restraining him
with seven locks
coded keys were

necessary
engraved yesterday
afternoon
to lock the chains –
his arms to the chains
and he is a
good lover who
bleeds for me
I have tested
all of my new
piercings
this time
and they work!

233

Illness strikes
a pain in the hip
a split lip
malaise
soreness
anguish
that battered feeling
that comes from
nothing but
lack of sleep
and long walks
after months of
no activity
has captured me
and settled in
my bones
my flesh aches
my tattoos are
slow in healing
I am not sure

how to deal
with this one
I could use a
portable hospital bed
a traction mobile
a supply of narcotics
but as these things
will not be granted
to me –
I will drag myself
around hoping
I can avoid using
the cane
even as my arm
spasms
from the pressure
of holding
a pen – my neck
cracks and shooting
pains fly through
my legs..

234

It is harder to
get in the bus
using a cane
I have had five days
off from work and
codeine pills with
no improvement
maybe when summer
comes my joints will
loosen in the heat
and I can walk unaided
again
I flop myself down

in the seat,
the vibration from
the dash not as
painful as slowly
lowering myself down
I flop myself down
like a dead mackerel
the aftereffects of
painkillers have
me nauseated
the jerking and
screeching of the bus
give no relief
I think myself
I am a faker, until
I try to walk
and the bones
scream out
I am not a faker
but wish I was
phoney limp
is
better than a
real one
any day

235

No long poem today
it was standing room only
until Catherine Street
The MTA has cut the number
of buses going to City Hall

For some unknown reason
the day will be warm

I conquered my fear of strange
places yesterday at Smitty's memorial
and again in bed, trying to find
a place to sleep under the aching
of my sorry bones
it feels like growing pains
but I guess it is the ungrowing
now that hurts
my arrival
at full blown decrepitation

No one said it would be this bad
to get old,
perhaps it is only a vitamin overdose
or lack of a companion dog
or medication overload
but my osseous structures are in revolt
they want to be in someone else's
body and I can't much blame them
because so would I.....

..... RIP Smitty 4/97

236

Dark day for starters
New York's Finest
is on the bus with us
no sleep for me
bum leg in anarchy
brain is buzz city
ears protesting with a high
pitched ringing
I don't need friends
I already got all the noise

anyone could want
swimming in the soup

No one I know died today yet
although there was a close call yesterday
everything looks the same as
it always does on a dark morning
people still run to their
appointed positions in the scheme
in the web   in the void
because if they are not present
at least 100,000 things will not happen.

Of course, that would only mean
they were not supposed to show up and
those 100,000 things that happened
99,999 different ways
(pure chance probably allows for
one repetition)
were not ordained to occur
in the usual manner

I thank all the powers
that right now
in this instant in time
in the middle of East Broadway
rounding the Worth Street turn
that this bus is supposed to be
clean, intact, peaceful and full
of living passengers
including me

237

Bright visions
are the trees
in the playgrounds

in the mini parks
and the median strips
along Houston Street
suddenly after the storm
they appear
like new mushrooms
in the lawn
as if they were not there
yesterday
it is still so cold
in the morning
I like it that way
it seems more like Autumn
bright sunshine however
should be banned until noon
intensifying as it does,
the brilliance
of the spring trees
to a crescendo
that sears my guts
with memories
of other spring times
of young vicious lovers
of the dead ones
and all the rest
a flood is in progress
there are leaks
in the dams
and the trees
the trees
are suddenly green

238

I know from the blinding sunlight
I have arrived too late
this is nothing new

I believe that I may have to
lose some pierces
I don't want this to happen
I like being full of artificial holes
but the tongue is not healing as it should
the pubic bleeds occasionally
and probably needs a shorter bar

A flock of pigeons flies
across the street
like in the wild
don't they realize they are
in NYC and they are supposed to walk?

I have two infections
cursing my body
at all times
but always with different locations
last week it was my lower lip
now it is my left nostril
and the base of my spine
I don't know where they come from
or why they take so long to leave

I am hungry
the bus passengers are probably
hungry for their morning
roll and coffee
I am hungrier than that

everything looks clean up here today
but that is why the subways
are full of garbage
they wanted to hire welfare people
to clean for them
but the deal fell through
so we will stay knee deep
in rotten misery

which appears to be right where
the majority of us belong

239

"Delancey Street"
announces our driver
a second after I get on the bus
PA 4302
the day is brilliant
a sparkling edge
a glint of hubcap
the trees are pristine
in the bath of clear light
sun glare is causing accidents
out on the highways
another hint of beauty's
inherent danger
the Trade Center towers
glow above the bridge
that goes over Chinatown
not one speck of garbage
on the street anywhere
we pull in at Chatham Square
faced with gleaming cars
all shining like new cadillacs
the pigeons are forlorn with
only a few measly bread crumbs
to peck
Dr. Toothy's red neon advertisement
at the corner signals
arrival at Worth Street
The Federal Building is still there
and I have somehow made it
into the beginning of
another adventure

240

My view from the bus window
is clouded
by raindrops
and morning eye maladjustment
It is a cold one
people have been arguing
about the frigidness
"It is not supposed to
last so long," some say
"Oh yes," others dispute
I believe it lasts until mid-June
when I will finally feel safe
leaving home without a jacket
Memorial Day has always been
my marker and it does stay cold
in the mornings until
Summer Solstice

The white trucks lining Allen Street
are all stained gray by winter and
have not yet been washed for Spring
I feel gray
each winter harder as the years pass
each one felt more deeply in the bones
I can't wait to kiss this one good-bye
so I can begin my complaints
about the heat

241

A fine cool dappled day presents itself
for my enjoyment
I will try
though it will be hard

on three hours of sleep and
on an aching leg
no quiet night at home for me

I went first to the piercing shop
which was sold out of 10 gauge barbells
then into a severe asthma attack
home for the inhaler
back out to Blockbuster for
the Rodney Dangerfield movie
then to bind my lover in leather
restraints, locks and chains
and feed him pizza like a dog
shave him
eat ice cream from his body
for desert
notice that he is very heavy
in the gut for a twenty-four year old

He arrived in a suit
straight from his work at Radio Shack
When I remove his sneakers
I see he has painted his toenails
a desired shade of red
he is a secret of a man
extreme genital piercings
and four tattoos
I move his nipple ring
to his tongue
he will change it back tomorrow
which is today

I am hurt all over
from the extensive shaving
I had done in order to
take a photo of him in
spike stilettos for the cover
of my magazine

flashes of this shooting
fire off in my brain
as I arrive in downtown
Manhattan
in a near coma
this is the last devotion
Lance, who no longer cries,
his mother who has begun to nod her
head in my direction
and I must get off now
and begin the next phases
of our lives

Desecration #1

The 4 inch high stilettos
are empty
lying on their sides
askew
set off by the hardwood floor
they are size 10
and have been used
only three times
they are not mine
he paid $75.00 for them
on his plastic
and has left them
on my floor
they are too small for him
and yesterday
as I strapped them
on him
nude restrained
in ropes and chains
he said
"they feel good

when they are tight"

Why is the sound of a tongue
piercing banging on
a penis crucifix
made of two barbells
crisscrossing its head
so exciting?

It is no more than the sound
of marbles rotating
in someone's hand
or clear crystal stones
fall into a glass
vase
it is no more than that

2

My long red nails
my pen
the sun
early morning quiet
on the bus
almost can hear
the constant ear ringing
but it is nicely masked
by the MTA motor purr
cigarettes
exhaust pipes
accessories
implements to produce
the necessary evil
counterpoint
to a gorgeous day
hip pain is stilled

for the moment
our driver honks
a hilo operator
with a horn
that could blow him
right off his yellow
metal seat
I imagine my father's
John Deere tractor
maybe the hilo guy
believes with all his heart
that it is the bus driver's
duty to avoid him
and not the other way
around
the methadone clinic
does a brisk business
I don't need any
I have taken the prescribed
dose of codeine
the nausea begins
to creep into my throat
I don't like it much
will spend the rest of this ride
praying for better times

3

I will need some shoes
black
stiletto heel
5 inches or more
thin straps around
the ankle
to hold in that snake
tattoo

size 10 is too
small
the price too high
but that's
the tag on pleasure
his feet will look,
so pretty
and he will be
unable to take
a step

4

NO!
I do not need to run my hands
over your shaved skin
so badly
that I will become
a circus dog for it
I am not so thrilled with the
sight of that snake tattoo
when bound and partially
hidden behind the tightened
straps of black stilettos
that I will be satisfied
with your silence
you will answer my questions
now or you will be banished
NO!
I will not bathe you with
the attentions of my tongue
and it's cut zirconia piercing
jewelry
without the sound of moaning
you give only your body
but it is not enough for

me
I am looking for someone
who will welcome me to
carve my name across his chest
and who will make a gift
of pain to this love

5

my wild heart has been made
a doormat for the last time
tricked by Darla,, my man,
who comes dressed as little
red riding hood but slashes
deep with the fangs of a wolf.

I am back here inside my walls
and from within will battle
bravely
the Valkyrie in me leaps up
but I will not eat his body
I will leave it for the Vulture
Girls to have at him deliriously.

6

A glow in the East
hides the coming fury
decisions demand attention and
will not allow
a lingering to savor
the mysterious future,

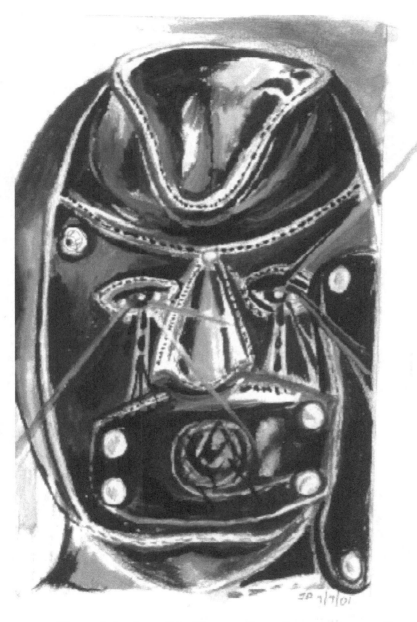

Graphic by JD Rage for the cover of
Thad Rutkowski's prose collection
Sex-Fiend Monologues II (Venom Press 2001)

Some one has asked me
if the name Rage
has some significance
does it symbolize
for example
a hatred of men
I say no
I love men
and do not elucidate
with my inner comment
"but I am no longer
sure why"

he wishes to sleep in
a cage
I survey the bedroom to see
if there is space for this
aspiring dogboy

If he supplies the cage
I can squeeze it in
a small one
where he will curl
up on his side
the drawback to this
arrangement:
no one to sleep in my bed
to warm me and caress
my demons to sleep.

7

There may be a slave trade
depending on whether
the new guy is satisfactory
Saturday will tell all

and with luck, the boy
will remove his things
with alacrity and return
my keys
he thinks
I
want a deep discussion
but all I really want is those
little metal things that
cost a twelve dollar
non-refundable
without the return of
the key deposit
that's it
he is off my list
for admitting deliberate
evasionary tactics
he was being pulled in too
many directions
and it is my direction
it seems
that is always the first to go
but now he will learn that
elimination is elimination
I am gone
he has been terminated
and can fasten his own stockings
from now until he
arrives in the hereafter

8

frozen face
like a tv dinner
cold to the heart
piercing early gray

Mother sends a card
for the holiday
although she won't call me
when I am in the hospital
she is a frigid fish
a headslap in all her
glorious power
she can reduce me to
shivering insignificance
from 200 miles away
or more
who could reduce her like that?
she learned it somewhere
to cut to slice
to chop
and I have no canvas
over which to wreak domination

a strong person is needed
who is like myself a challenge
there are few who would qualify
I have studied mind control
at the feet of a Master
who will probably grip me
well beyond the grave

9

Mean
yes that is me
cruel and evil
all because I want my keys
this seems to be a capital offense
a crime against the heart
oh keys
they are the most important thing

and that's the way it is
so be it
yes so be it then
after being shut off/out ignored
and eradicated
so easily and without
thought desire or longing
then yes the keys
a metal arrangement
a real thing
that you can touch and feel
and will open your door
a thing that is costly to replace
and difficult to do without
my keys are all that remain
the objects of my unending love
I want them back in my pocket
in my knapsack
in my drawer
not in yours
you don't need them
you don't want them
so give them back
and while you are at it
remove those X-rated Polaroids
you have somehow become
an angel
and no one wants to be
reminded of when
you were human

10

The birds again whirling across the sky
the bus is late
a survey has revealed that

only three passengers go to City Hall
at 7:00 in the morning
so they have cut
the number of buses to one
but there is a grand secret
made of when it will come
usually it is pulling out
before you have
effectively presented yourself
at the curb for carting
so wait in the cold
under the gulls
who seek food and
are not rewarded with a banquet

we are all
waiting for something
    a bus
    a meal
    a lover
    a casket
    a scattering of ashes

I stand near the stove
and watch the pot
to prove the fallacy of the
adage "a watched pot never boils"
of course it isn't true
but one must wait
even after the tiny bubbles
begin to surface
one must wait
even after the first large ones
break through
one must wait
until the water
arrives at a full rolling boil
then you can make your tea

or prepare your lo-cal Jell-O
or reduced sugar hot chocolate

and only then
can one satiate the desire
that led to the boiling of water

desire: the cup of tea
is quickly consumed
and the whole procedure
will be repeated
it may be better
not to watch
I find oblivion
to be an excellent substitute for patience.

11

Nobody keeps their word any more
so why do I?
The doctors don't
do what they tell you they will
they don't care if you are in dire straits
If you should die –
it is one less millstone-
one less albatross around their neck.
The ex-boyfriend doesn't come through
in his pledge to return the keys.
Oh so keys are all you care about he says
so be it he says
at least I care about something
I conclude
after being held prisoner
in my apartment
for three evenings waiting
for someone who says he will

be there and never appears
And keys?
leave keys with a man who
deliberately does not speak with you
for no reason that makes any sesnse
If the keys were his he would be worse
than I am
with someone he didn't trust
It is not just the doctor and boyfriend
though they are the best examples

who can you trust
are you as bad as the rest
you can't be the only good person left

Conclusion –
there are <u>no</u>
persons to
be
trusted.
Not even me!

12

Pesky sunshine glares through
my dark glasses
doesn't it know I am a vampyre
bat and will easily melt?

My Domination dreams of bondage
and control diminish with
the latest meeting
an unworthy male who displays his
favorite paddle before vanishing
without a trace

I must be a total ogre for them to blow away
like so much insignificant quivering dust
I never imagined that they wouldn't like me
I would be the one to pick and choose
an egotistical assumption
for they do not like me
not even skinny
not in six inch high heels an a micro mini

I guess it must be the ghost of my fangs
sharp phantoms, removed when they tried
to make my teeth look normal
but the essence of the piercing
feeling of bone sinking into soft flesh
that is what scares them
invisible but effective
I guess it must be the ghost of my fangs
those pearly apparitions make even the
pain puppies run away holding their necks
so that I might not consume them
whole on the hoof
and they will not return
I guess it must be the ghost of my fangs
not a one of them has the nerve
to take such a massive risk

13

I

And so I have arrived at another
holiday season
alone
to celebrate by myself

a Halloween spent in the
pulmonary ward
listening to the night noises
of the nursing home contingent
who reduce the werewolf howl to
a tabby cat meow
with their moaning
sounds escape them constantly
with no control
as if a dying wildcat was trapped
inside their chests
and they lay there
like putty
with half a face
mouth propped open
with tubes for breathing and feeding
looking like a perfect wide "O"
the mouth of Popeye's little baby Sweetpea
no definition to the appearance
no features
no use for the voice
and who is this sad specimen
of a lady
who is set into moan motion by a
cruel blood test drawn from non-existent
veins
who was she before
the cigarettes did her in
a cigarette she would not now recognize
right under her nose
and hasn't for several years
who is this tragedy
who spoils my sleep
whose cadence is the background
to my tiptoed looking out the
fourth story window of
Linsky Building over the
scary air vents carrying

the incubus of every known disease
in its hideous flow
much scarier than the
All Hallows Eve costumes
on the street below

For some reason they are all
dressed as doctors, nurses, derelicts
and bums
very convincing too
but where are the skeletons and vampires?
the presidents and other thieves?
I see not a one on this evil evening
I see only my future dying in a lonely bed
unaware that she is observed by

the present
which will soon be the past

II

I am alone
scanning First Avenue
waiting in vain for the arrival
of a 4 wheel drive truck whose owner
has promised a visit

Tomorrow is Thanksgiving
I have no boyfriend, no liaison, no slave
to cook my turkey
I haven't even got a date
I have scared him away too
he who says he admires my kind
I am too real
It seems too obvious that I will control
you no matter what the price
so I will spend Christmas #13

in solitude
I had hope this year for a change
some kind of miracle
but no
it is the same old
"You have a beautiful smile"
a sugary euphemism for
"drop dead you ugly old hag"
the prelude to never uttering
another word in my direction

I receive gifts that I don't want
and accept them out of kindness
then get ignored for my trouble.

14

Everyone who was missing
has resurfaced
with allegedly valid explanations
but still lying about
their true intentions
it doesn't matter
there is a new belle
who calls himself
crawling mud man
in abbreviated initials thereof
I am sure it is a popular name
in cyber reality
he is a cynic
a grande paranoid
and is very cute in a dress
so for the time being
--while we have not met--
it is a bright burning flame
between us

I wonder what reason this one
will find to not adore me--
he thinks he is unique
and doesn't realize
he is simply a garden variety
dime-a-dozen budding crossdresser
his fantasies of his difference
from the rest of humanity
so precious to him
what is making them all tumble out
wishing for petticoats and corsets
and lace undergarments of their own
beneath their business clothes?
Something in the moon?
A femme fatale wrinkle in the void?

I am told that women like me
who delight in such men as if they were
our own private
walking talking 5 o'clock shadowed
Barbie dolls --
are rare
A lot of Dominants
will put up with anything
for money
but this is not for the cash
this is for the lust
the pure desire of it

there is now shortage of raw materials
who want to dress up and serve tea
and take their punishment like good
little boygirltoys
but why will this mud man crawl away?
One found me too old
one became overwhelmed with guilt
and wiped off his ravishing red lipstick
at the thought that his dead brother

could see what he was doing
One wanted a woman who enjoyed her

alcohol and so hopefully
would not notice
while locking him in a cage
that he enjoyed his
this one seems like a treasure
a dream
to mold in my own way
but I will not hold my breath
for the miracle
that claims to be
waiting

15

I have finally out done Humpty Dumpty's
greatest fall
on a straight flat even sidewalk yet,
who needs a prop like a wall,
my ankle turned and introduced
the hard cement to my delicate face
I broke a blood vessel in my palm
I looked like Jesus after the nail
on impact I thought my skull had shattered
but I have a hard head and brains like scrambled
eggs
It will take more than a short free fall to
the pavement
to conquer me
although on rising feebly
picking up my jettisoned glasses
and my now flattened gold earring
I couldn't help but ask if I was being
punished

I told the scared little schoolboys
who thought they were going to witness death
that I was fine
Their shocked eyes told me they lacked
confidence
in the truth of my reply

I staggered home more careful now
not to drop into the path of an oncoming vehicle
I guess I was luckier than my counterpart Humpty
who lost his kingdom and being a flimsy omelet
ingredient
could not get up and go home
there will be no rotten egg smell in my wake
but I still wonder if I am being punished
or perhaps I am being called
or maybe it is a simple matter of a voodoo spell

16

I imagined I would be a good choice
for difficult characters, but the new applicant
is another paranoid and takes valium
this is before meeting me
he thinks I will hurt him
blackmail him expose him on national tv
chain him up and leave him to die
or not really be what I say I am
just some old girl who can't get a
boyfriend any other way

Too many little worries
too many nervous conditions
too many doubts
too much value placed on looks

and visits to the gym
and he is good at contamination
I have decided that yes, I do want a slave
because I can't get a boyfriend any other way
I am a real loser
if that is the case
because domination is a lot harder
than vanilla dating
I don't like my image as it is reflected
back to me by this man
I don't like being recreated in the
colors of his fear
he is ashamed to call me
Mistress
he is unable to accept himself as he is

I guess difficult characters are no longer
a good choice for me
the complexity rating here is well beyond my
talents
or desire to exceed present boundaries
I think I will return him to the pond
before he drowns me

17

I am tickling the
chrysalis - spun so
tightly a boy wrapping
himself up in
and adding layers
each decade til he
is nearly mummified
only eye, ear and
mouth openings remain
the other nerve

endings buried
in self denial
This is not me
and could not be me
and yet he calls
himself me
this hibernating
caterpillar
is wiggling inside
the shiny shroud
which enfolds him
pulling up his feet
to struggle
and he will emerge
under my guidance
his feet one at a
time, sheathed in
a black leather stiletto
shoe so that when
he caresses my ankles
we understand
each other
and then will be the
trembling of the wet
newborn continue
as the wind dries
him and he perches
on the milk weed
pod preparing to
try out his delicate
but powerful wings.

18

I am up and truly
disgusted to have
spent so much time

preparing only to ride
on this garlic express
I don't even have a
piece of gum to chew
to mask part of the
rotten breath smell
why did I brush my teeth
I will smell of putrid
rank stenchy digested
bile all day
And where is my chauffeur
to ferry me
through these lackluster
streets to my
hideous final distinction
oh it would not be
enough for me
no all the love
all the inhalables
all the sedative drugs
would not be enough
I am Elvis on the inside
I would eat 29 lbs
of mashed & gravy
until I gorged
and needed to
cart my belly in
a wheelbarrow
or a crane to hoist
me from my couch
sated never
always want more
riches wouldn't
appease me
I want more
I am better than this
I will sit in the
front seat and distribute

breath mints
to all the unsanitary riches

19

There is a great
relief when an
impending disaster
washes away
and your lover
still trusts you
even though at
your very core you are
schizo insane
seeing things two
or maybe three ways
at the same time
ways that are not
reconcilable
and sometimes may
appear to be delusional
self-effacing or
erasing
views that soften
reality to a warm
blur and when
contemplated
from the back
looking through them
on the blade
that pierces in from
the other side
they are cold
solid machine like
steel iron

immovable
and cold, cold, untouchable
protected.

A man in red panties,
red garter belt
black stockings with
a run
puffy chest from
lifting weights
is in the kitchen
washing dishes
at the end of a leash
playing in a girlish
way, impish
prancing pigeon-toed
in his black high heels
to him a clown in his
embarrassment
but to me a beauty
my toy

he is unsettled
unfamiliar with his
new role
but eager
insecure but more
secure than he has ever
been
quieting down
but still ready
to bolt -
I want to lock him
up and eat the
key.

I want to
commit Art Vice
paint & sketch
it
I see some on the
bus – a woman
all leather & dreads
silver rings
fake fingernails
and Rayban
clone shades
with the price
still on the earpiece
$3.99 -
I will create
portraits of the back
end of a boy
slavegirl in
bondage
presenting
his openness
to me and through
my paintings
to the world.
I need a pink bow
for the collar
I will mark him
with the crop
stake him out
wrap him up
guard & protect him
but I will also
display him
recognizable
features abstracted

But I will know
it is him
and he will know
and what if
there is a painting
and I don't like it?
- don't look at it he whispers
baybee
It is art vice
It can be seen
without it
using your eyes

21

I dressed him up
in a maid uniform
to cook and serve my
dinner
and after the makeup
was delighted to see
he looked like Johnny
Thunders without it
he resembled Cheetah
Chrome (when stripped
and from a certain angle)
better looking really
than either of them
since he doesn't
do hard drugs or
soft ones either
unless D/s is a soft
or hard drug
he doesn't
he looked like
Johnny a bit

but even more
like slave Missy's -
not much prancing
this time in those
5 inch spike stilettos
a beautiful boy/girl
kept saying
"I could pass for a girl
couldn't I?"
or "I don't think
I could pass for a girl,
could I?"
He could pass in
a dress, shave, wig
right for his coloring,
blond, not black
because he is slim
and has pretty legs
"I am a good looking
person" he said, "I don't
think of myself as
a good looking person"
I said "you'll do"
"I could never pass for
a girl, my nose is too
big"
"Oh girls don't have
big noses?"
"You are too pretty
to be a girl"
he told me
"too pretty to be
a girl"
- this is why for
most of the evening
slave wore
a leather gag.

He is more like a
butterfly than I ever
imagined
a small one, not
a majestic monarch
or tiger swallowtail
or even a deathshead
moth
now he is more a
yellow sulfur or
a white cabbage
butterfly
delicate
my fingers smeared
with shiny powder
from his wings
after capturing him
and he tries to fly
with the coloration
now transparent
I do not attempt
to pull off his legs
but they being
so fragile might
break before my best
intentions
a butterfly or lepidoptera's
life is short
and frenzied
I know what I
want but
he is a simple
bug with no lucidity
To see if he is mine,
I will let him

go
that is the only
logical
path.

23

It is Christmas Eve
last night I heard
on TV that there
was no trace of
the Virgin Mary on
this earth, no grave
marker, no remains
I see this as meat
for future archaeological
expeditions
Today I will
travel with donkeys
and wind up not
in a stable but
an office building,
a far less useful
structure
where paper flies with
abandon
less ordered than
a bed of hay
I will not think of
the true meaning
of Christmas
because I don't know
what it is
realizing immediately
that there was
no snow in

the desert
which immediately
causes confusion
for me.

24

Gorged but never
sated, I ride
downtown, heavy
with yesterday's fare
of turkey, stuffing,
gravy, mashed,
artichoke hearts,
green beans, corn
biscuits, apple &
pumpkin pie
it was so good
and I wanted more
it was never enough
again.
I might well have
done better to
fall on a sword
rather than suffer
the eventual diabolic
consequences of such
indiscretion
but I will not
do it again any time
soon
I have a new vice
a precious distraction
an artist's model
eager and
even greedy for
the brush

I can indulge with
no poisonous
effects if he will
only trust me
then I can do
anything.
I have left an
accidental mark,
a bruise
it makes him feel
like he belongs to
me
Oh tattoo gun
I would use your power
to make a general
announcement
inscribing my
name on
his trampy cheeks
and taking him
out to
moon
the masses.

25

It is nice outside
the bus window
cool, gray, romantic
with the mottled
sky suggesting the
imminent arrival
of fallen angels
my kind of atmosphere
I am happy for it
but bad weather is
approaching a nor'easter

in time for Charlene's
Anniversary which I
insist on attending
it will be wet
freezing and miserable
I am hoping it ends
before New Year's Eve
although I know
that stampeding
rhinos could not
keep slaveboy from
presenting on my
bed for his
punishment
my pleasure
I have planned it,
only these plans
of all the ones I make
come true
This slave says
he loves me
but it is just a test
to see what my
response will be
and when I say
you love the idea of
having a Mistress,
you don't love Mistress,
he laughs and calls
me difficult

26

A wild day is
in progress light
rain but big winds

blowing the Burger King
banner and the
smoke from the Con Ed
underground
construction pipes
and making its unseen
presence strikingly
visible
the modern decor
store obtrudes with
a bright pink
facade amid the
dingy tenements
aging graffiti
in pink wearing
down to gray
its creator in
prison now or
art school
I am a graffiti loving
person
Yes there is something
relaxing about a
clean shining building
also something
robotic, inhuman,
sanitized.
The graffitied trucks
in Chinatown are
the best, bright
blue and red lettering
breaks the monotony
of white paneling
dirty looking even
when clean
The writing complements
well the Chinese
lettering on the

restaurants, herbalist
and bridal stores
I once was a graffiti
artist and even photographed
my last inscription
before its demise
It stayed put for
many years before
a new bar came
and painted it out
to announce its own
name: King Tut's
Wah Wah Hut.
My graffiti, My
band Baby Boom,
the club we played in
The A-7 on 7th St
and Avenue A are
all gone, dead, and
forgotten - a pity -
especially the graffiti
that lives its
art out in the streets in
public

27

New Year's Eve
what a party
I was privileged
with the offer
of a body
living of course
to which I could
do anything
including total

transformation into
a creature
completely new
that has not existed
before except in dreams
to be recreated
instantaneously at my
whim
an immobile bound
and beautiful
monster was made
by me at my
party of 2 on
N.Y.E.
who when directed
presented to me
a canvas of
white backside
on which I painted
words in blue
red orange and yellow
and flogged
them off then
spanked off the remnants
of those words
I made love to my
monster
I let it bite me
I watched him in his
mangled glory
and wanted to
invent him
until
he could stand
no more

28

Is the dogbowl
cat a happy one
sporting a green
wig
and green eye shadow
will it meow
louder than any
alley feline
fornicator
or will the
pussy be immobilized
chained hand
and foot to
the chrome drawer
handles of
a wooden platform
bed
yowling as the
miniature whip
crisscrosses
his kitty cat
jewels
sending his
restless male
essence off to sleep
in quiet heavens
while his ladylike
heart remains to
be tenderly
tortured
by the hand
that coaxed
it out into the
here and now
meow

she is here now
meow
the bondage prissy
and her
beautiful confiner
meow
the cat with the
dog tags
drinks and lives
to tell about it.

29

Boredom seems like an excellent option today
my medications have all combined in a way
that rivals and amplifies the foggy weather

At the stop, someone asks me for the time
I get annoyed as usual
since I am now obligated
to lift my hand from my pocket,
twist my wrist and focus my eyes
not to mention moving my mouth
in a semi-pleasant manner

There next to the bodega,
are a small Hispanic couple
with a baby

And here comes the bum
a tall man who appears
to be dressed normally until I see
his shoes
ill-fitting, no laces
high-topped with tongues flapping
he is alone near a huge pile of
cardboard to be recycled

he searches his pocket for money
and seems to find some,
a coin appears to drop
he searches the sidewalk with rheumy eyes
and suddenly he is no longer alone
searching in the exact spot
where everyone must pass
the street comes alive with people, bicycles
and strollers, all trampling
through the place where the derelict looks
for his imaginary money.

Later on the bus
I learn the woman who needed the time
is going to an interview
and feel happy I helped to ease her mind
the baby was quiet and slept
for the whole trip

30

The warm fog
shrouds everything
in this January heatwave
and I am depressed
everyone who has
a heart already loves
someone else with it,
someone who isn't right
for them, someone
who has left or they
have given up
My interval between
men is 14 years
with 3 minor flings
and I no longer love

anyone – maybe it
was easier for me
because I was a
different person then
and the men were
dreadful messes
but now I have found
a better quality
a man with depth
I hoped was free
free from old strings
loose from bad loves
escaped from nature's
drives
clear and beautiful
but he isn't –
he loves a woman
who he describes as
"not so smart",
she lives in his building
he manages her affairs
together for several years
there was not enough
to talk about
and so he left
it was unpleasant
sad, tragic and
he still wants
babies –
now she has found
a new lover
and he is in turmoil
she told him they
will be friends.
I wonder who is
not so smart
me for sure
involving a small

part of my soul
again with a man
who loves another –
him most likely
for forbidding
himself the thing
he loves for
stupid reasons
for this we probably
belong together
but it seems
unlikely, even though
there will always be
something to talk about

31

I am now on the evening
bus the M-9 from
WTC to Union Square
It has been a balmy
day in the high
sixties in January
Almost like Spring
and I have the fever
and I am dreaming
of beauty
all innocence and delight
prancing in a black
wig
the strands of fake
hair going in her
mouth unless clipped
back with a thick
barrette
I am seeing beauty
undress and dress for

me at my pleasure
here in my blue
plastic bus seat
I am envisioning
my beauty
superimposed
on the predominantly
Asian riders
as they board in
Chinatown
I know they are
what is really before
my eyes
but I am picturing
beauty
transformed into
a living X
in her ropes
and chains
a mask tied around
her eyes
a red ball protruding
from her perfect
mouth
It is dark out
and all the neon
Chinese lettering
makes a glittering background
for my visions
It could be schizophrenia
it could, I think, as I imagine
her kneeling in
the pink bow I have
tied to her collar
kneeling beside me
here in the bus
my faithful servant
girl, It is so real

I lay down my pen
and caress her face
it is rough, the way
I like it
and also smoothed by
my imagination
we are riding home
on this city bus
I have a tight grip
on her leash
but then I look
down and see only
a grooved black rubber
floor speckled with
white to hide the
fact that gum blobs
have been permanently ground
into it.
It could be schizophrenia
I guess
that must be what
it is.

32

You feel so good
because you just got laid,
he said on the phone
and I winced at the crude nature of men
even of compliant types
who like to be overpowered
by demanding tyrant valkyries
even those helpless bound maidens
are still vulgar masculine creatures
who need to be beaten
all crass remarks will be registered
on the punishment list

that unseen document that grows
more lengthy with every
inappropriately raised eyebrow
every ludicrous vocal inflection
every moronic thoughtless stray
remark like that one

but then he said
you feel good
because you made love
and that was what it was you know, he said
I know, I said,
silently deducting a few strokes from
my disciplinary plan

33

I like this day
it is a cold wet one
or rather dampish
as no rain at the moment
the air however
feels like a fresh cool
splash of spring water
and after yesterday
a monsoon would
be a relief
I am no longer in
possession of a slaveboy
he has let his contract
lapse.
I will see him Saturday
for renegotiation
I don't know why I
want my piece of
parchment laser paper
to lock in my

security file
signed by him
to agree that I am
his owner
that his sex belongs
to me,
the skin of his
upper back
his chest with
clothespins dangling
his cute face
my beauty
no longer is
exclusively
mine
I am nobody's
Mistress today
except my own
the most difficult
slave of all
to control - -

34

On the kitchen table
I saw the barrette
you used to tie back
your black hair
and I was drenched
in visions of
you
in the bathtub
like a sweet little boy
ready to be
washed clean of
the cares of life

the worries of the future
at the sink
preparing food
delighted to be useful
in white stockings tight
garter and nothing
else
on the floor reading
to me during my
meal
on my lap
my sexy baby doll
in the living room
protected by my
strength
wrapped around my
body on the couch
in the bedroom
vulnerable
facing danger
to please me
in the bathroom
washing up
my house is filled
with after images
of your
shades of your
echoes

35

Here comes that old devil weight again
meaning it is definite that I like him
Yes. I like him,
so I will chub out
get bigger adding a pound a day

I have already put on 6.5 instead of losing 8
as I had planned
I am sure I can push him away
though I am not sure weight is going to work
this time
he is not that shallow
fat fat fat fat
has its advantages
fills out my face
diminishing the cracking wrinkles
of old age
but the drawbacks are far greater
this has got to stop now
or I will die
what is the sense in committing
suicide
to avoid being attractive
to one who has captivated me
oh so then I can always say
it was I who rejected him
before he turned sour
but I can't do these things anymore
a diabetic can not screw around with sugar
on non-stop eating extravaganzas
so if I want to live
if I want to stick around here as long as I can
I must dredge back up the will to survive
that elusive force
oh baybee oh baybee
don't you know that
happiness is not poison
it will not kill you
there is some small element
of self-protection from the hypnotic
effect of pleasure
going on amid the overriding act
of self-removal
these are the things to watch out for

a schizophrenic will investigate every
opposing angle to avoid a cure
and will hear every little morsel
begging Eat me Eat me.

36

Up till now, I was an invisible
disabled person
who could at times be very ill
but nothing showed
and no one believed me
either

Now I have been caned.
I have a nice one that my father made
but I still don't like it
try to bring a friend birthday presents
in the rain
try to carry home your shopping
and see what fun it can be

all this leg stuff
no feeling and drop foot on the left
arthritic hip on the right
is compounded by a bad right arm
tennis elbow it is called
though I have never played
tennis
but have played bass guitar for years
so I have punk rock bass player's elbow
which often requires wearing
two restrictive braces
to keep things from moving around
so try reaching into your pocket
for your bus pass

while carrying an umbrella and a bag
in your left hand while caning
with the damaged right
and dragging your braced left
leg up the steps which the bus
driver lowers only after you have
reached the top

there is no consolation prize
but to be entitled to the disabled seats
at the front, which are always filled
with able-bodied types who won't budge
and if lucky, and finally seated
places one at the mercy of the other
passengers who seem to take perverse delight
in smashing us in the knees with their heavy metal
packages

37

The reason for my name has started
to seethe in my cauldron
I am a rattlesnake
coiled and hissing
I am a rabid wolf
growling low and baring
my yellow teeth

people always say they don't wish to hurt me
and for some reason the only way they
can accomplish this desire
is to leave me in the desert
crawling
is to walk away before the show begins
is to reject my advances as if to
approach me was to jump in a vat of superglue

is to shut themselves off from my
irresistible influence

and so yes
I am a pariah
thundering in forests where no one
can hear or see me fall

will I scrape myself up once more
and throw myself in the path
of another hapless victim
or will I stay down and leave
the world in peace?

38

I awoke from the lecture dream
recalling that it was certainly not as bad
as the worm dream
in that there were no genitals
or writhing maggots on display
only droning from which I was
more than happy to escape into this
dark early morning

the bus will be downtown
in a matter of minutes
there is no traffic to cause delays
the only thing that could stop us
is a bus driver heart attack
but he appears quite healthy and all
this leads me to suspect
that I will be going through the
door at work
in less than ten minutes

it is dress down Friday
the only day
I have the desire
to jump from my bed
and get trucking

39

Yesterday was 2/2/98
19 years after the tragic death
of Sid Vicious
five more days will mark
the rebirth of someone who thought
she was Sid reincarnate
and who was pushing the future
past, present
shatterings of his soul
to join themselves
all on one side of eternity
all on the same side
that being the dead side

the joyous reemergence
of someone who had buried herself
so far down
drowned in elixirs and concoctions
that she could no longer summon
her own return
could no longer
align the transparent planes
in harmony

It has taken thirteen years
to apply the glue
using it to hold things together
instead of sniffing it

inside a plastic bag
I wonder how much longer it
will take to dry?

40

Lover boy toy is
not dreaming
there are wookies
on my bus
with strange
non-human markings
we pass all
the restaurants on
Allen Street
that I wish I
had been able to
go
In the Hellfire
Club with my pet
we will talk
with other Mistresses
Big Fat Ones
of massive poundage
who hate themselves
and their sluts
burley hairy men
dressed in leather
skirts and dingy
lace blouses
who hate themselves
This is the ruling
and if so
do we also
HATE OURSELVES
or is it just the

way I feel meshes
with those
who may not be
so happy with the
skin they are in
but I thought that
my problem
was
I HATE EVERYONE
with few exceptions
that is
I LOVE anyone who
has tried to remove
this thorn from my
paw
the denizens of
the S&M club
want to insert more
thorns
Can I talk to them
to get an audience
for my own
scenes
with my little
Frankenstein doll?
where he will
kneel beside
me in his
crotchless panties
and serve his
Mistress
sweetly?

41

The gulls from the East River
perch on the tall street lamps
along Houston Street this morning
watching me as I walk along
they don't know what I have done
or what else I am capable of doing
or that I feel my power surging
I am a Conquistadora

I think a hood that laces up the back
with a snap-on blindfold and gag
is a very fine accessory
though it may be costly, there is
a deep peaceful beauty
in enforced leather silence

42

A man smashes his head against a wall
instead of hitting me
that's all I remember of the nightmare
this most recent one also features
a faceless figure berating me for
the size of my stomach

All my dreams are like this
it is a blessing that I mostly don't
recall them
it is enough to be under seige in daylight
no nocturnal repetition or escalation is required
the night is for resting
dreams are for fantasy

all troubles to vanish in the sandman's twinkling
dust
I want to make love to hunky movie stars
but instead I eternally endure my unconscious
mirror's egotistical attempts to demolish me

43

Full moon
Friday the 13th
and Valentine's Day all in one week
could be a bit much to handle
especially when your vision care plan
won't give you glasses
your boss steps up his humiliation tactics
and the phone is silent for long blocks
of time
I hate the phone
and I love the phone
typical of
the twisted multiplicity
of my simultaneous but
opposing feelings
I hate the city
I love the city
I hate people
but I love them madly
I hate food
but .....
heh heh
as I always say,
who would want cake
if they couldn't eat it too?

44

The toys are gathering dust
the whips no longer sing
my body keeps on walking
I feel my mouth still moving
and my eyes don't stop their looking
all the clocks insist on ticking
even though the reason
to know the time is gone
the phone is hideous tones of silence
someone has ordered it not to ring
not to echo the sound of heavy mourning
while the tears have dried upon my cheek
and the kiss is just a memory
The wings have all been folded
no more flying will be done

45

things are very flat but tolerable
I forgot to call my daddy on birthday No. 80

He was mad
I could hear it
his voice was lower
as if he was imitating the low voice
of my brother
who paid him a personal visit
to Florida, driving from the State
of Washington
driving one step ahead of an el nino storm
but I called
one day late
having been mired in the throes of desecration

and I know my Dad would not wish
to talk to me at all
if he knew who I really was
all my tattoos
all the piercings
and my penchant for dressing men up
like frilly barbie dolls
to watch them do the things
that men will do
but outfitted in trappings so flimsy
and impractical
a real woman would never agree
to wear them

47

I am confused about everything
can't seem to isolate the problem
I guess than means
I am the problem
too much work and no fun makes JD
a dull girl
I will interview a potential slaveboy tonight
without much enthusiasm
he is 46 years old and wants to be a girl
he is a chubette
from the photographs he has sent
he looks just like my first husband's
old Jewish battle-ax of an iron-willed mother
but he says he is a JAP and has a pretty smile
I am fed up with phony sissy boys
and this one may suffer from my
recent bad experiences
my patience is gone
If he can't cook

he is doomed
I was nasty to another guy because
he liked my poetry
I am such a mean bitch
I don't ever believe them when they say
that anyway because none of them have
the concentration it takes to read a simple poem
I guess I will have to change my haircolor again
maybe that will be the solution.

from a self-portrait color Polaroid
converted to gray

About JD Rage

J.D. Rage (1947-2018) said she dreamed herself up in a drug rehab in 1978 and came to life in February of 1985 on the sixth anniversary of the suicide of Sid Vicious. She believed that words are more important for their sound than their conventional meaning but that when both effects combine in harmony, the result is true beauty.

While searching for excitement and peace, she played bass guitar and sang lead in several bands - The Bandits, The Line-Up, Valkyries, and Disciples of Rage, among others - and Baby Boom, with whom she recorded the 1984 EP *Basket Case* [Rant Records V2279] She wrote three unpublished novels, painted many portraits, and worked with film and digital photography.

JD was co-editor of *CURARE*, a multimedia magazine put out by Venom Press, which she co-founded with Jan Schmidt. Together they published chapbooks by Larry Jones, Bruce Weber, Thaddeus Rutkowski, Susan Sherman, David Huberman and others. JD Rage was one of the co-hosts of the Sunday Open Series at ABC No Rio in New York in the 1990's. Some of the poems in this book were first published in *Stained Sheets*, the irregular journal of that "unorganized reading". Besides her seven chapbooks, JD had poems published in *Downtown Poets* (1999) from Montclair Takilma Books [ISBN 9 780966 936711] and *Anthology ABC No Rio Open Mike 1987* [ISBN 0-934911-01-2]

And all the while she was still Janet Whalen, Claims Manager at the State Insurance Fund down on Church Street. She had some of her paintings hanging in her office there. They didn't mind her being odd because she did her job so well, and she rose to a management position, tattoos and all, before declining health forced her early retirement.

JD Rage wrote in one of her bios, "She thinks Jack Kerouac is god even though it is no longer politically correct for a woman to feel that way. And by the way, god is dead. LUV, JD."

I am in a fog
of high blood sugar
my hangover from
yesterday's fling
with poor eating habits

my CD ROM drive
kept me up past
midnight
refusing to work
even after being fed
new software products

I felt so weird
in the night
I can't even describe it
but sort of like
I was a machine
made of metal
like this bus
and cold inside
like this morning
Easter is coming
a plane went down
last night
killing a close friend
of the president
all meetings conferences
and coup d'etat are
cancelled until
tomorrow

21

City Hall is smiling at me
her mouth is wide open
lit by spotlights
raised on eyebrows of
three draperies lined up in a row
over tall banks of windows
she sticks out her tongue
an imaginary red carpet tumbling
down granite stairs
between
toothy columns
In spite of how she mocks me
now
I think of all the dirty deals
corruption
maybe even plots to kill
she has harbored in her gut
In spite of her undesirable
history in a rough neighborhood
the golden glow
bathed in Nature's artistry
heightened by
the cold crisp atmosphere
makes her elegant
makes me wish she was something
I could be proud of.

22

Dark and cold Good Friday
little drops of rain a nuisance
on my glasses but not enough
to break out an umbrella